Mr. Potato Head vs. Freud

Also by Clint McCown

Novels

The Member-Guest

War Memorials

The Weatherman

Haints

Short Fiction

Music for Hard Times: New & Selected Stories

Poetry

Labyrinthiad

Sidetracks

Wind Over Water

Dead Languages

Total Balance Farm

The Dictionary of Unspellable Noises:
New & Selected Poems, 1975—2018

Mr. Potato Head vs. Freud

Lessons on the Craft of Writing Fiction

Clint McCown

Press 53
Winston-Salem

Press 53, LLC
PO Box 30314
Winston-Salem, NC 27130

First Edition

Cover design by Dawn Cooper

Library of Congress Control Number
2021950158

Printed on acid-free paper
ISBN978-1-950413-39-3

CONTENTS

Preface
Caveat Emptor

Most things have to be learned the hard way. Parents know this. You can tell a mule-headed boy it's dangerous to climb onto the roof of a house, but the kid won't really believe it until the moment he hits the ground. I speak from experience—not as the parent in this particular scenario but as the mule-headed boy.

Similarly, when my cousin Doug told the six-year-old me not to stick a fork in a wall outlet, I demanded to know why, and he gave me an elegantly simple reason: *Because electricity is faster than you are.* What could be more clear? And yet I had my doubts. I was pretty fast, after all. Was electricity really faster than me? My doubts persisted right up until—well, I'll let you finish the story of how it played out, because this happened so many decades ago that the details have become a little blurry to me.

So believe me when I tell you I understand what it's like to be skeptical when a writing teacher tells you something you should or shouldn't do in your writing. For many of us, myself included, the tendency is to want to do the very thing we're told not to do. If someone says it's crazy to write a novel without using the letter *e,* someone will try it. In fact, that particular gimmick has been pulled off twice. Ernest Vincent Wright wrote the 50,000-word novel *Gadsby* in 1939, accomplishing his task by tying down the *e* stroke on his typewriter so no inadvertent use of the vowel would slip into the manuscript. Then French novelist George Perec repeated the feat, writing *La Disparition* in 1969—translated into English as *A Void.* Few would argue that these two parlor-trick novels are great literature, but they did what they set out to do, which was their only point.

Writers, I suspect, are largely contrarian by nature. We do tend to be misfits, after all, the outside observers, the ones who critique the status quo. That's because the very nature of true art is revolutionary. Writers as dissimilar as Rainer Maria Rilke and Ursula K. Le Guin have insisted that the message of all art is the same: *You must change your life.* The poet Wallace Stevens told us plainly that *Poetry is a destructive force.* And as I once read on a tee-shirt, *Good art won't match your sofa.*

These three claims about art are essentially the same. Each tells us that artists are here to rock the boat, to break the rules of what's expected. So break the rules.

But on the other hand, if you're reading this, you must have an interest in learning how to write more effectively, and to that end, there must be rules, principles, guidelines to follow. And therein lies the conundrum. If art is about blazing new territory, how can there be a map to take you there? If art is at its core a rule-breaking proposition, how can there be rules to teach you how to break them? How can originality be organized?

That's the tension between self-expression and communication. Self-expression needn't be bound by rules, but communication must be. Yes, art is a personal and unique manifestation of self-expression. But at the same time, art that doesn't communicate itself is failed art. We need to learn how to package our art properly so that neither self-expression nor communication is sacrificed. That's a tough balancing act.

And that's where teachers come in. Your job as the artist is to come at art through the purity of self-expression, while the teacher's job is to come at it from the other side, which is communication. In other words, the teacher's role is to help you say whatever it is you want to say. It isn't your artistic vision a teacher should be messing with, it's your delivery system. That's a tricky territory to navigate on both sides. Some would-be writers are too defensive to listen, which is understandable, since there can be a lot of ego invested in a page of free-flowing self-expression. But even the willing student can have a difficult time of it. It takes a certain degree of blind faith to listen to any teacher, especially if that teacher is telling you to fix something you may not even have realized was broken.

What I want to do in this book is address the most pervasive creative writing problems I've encountered over the past five decades of studying, teaching, and practicing the craft. These are all issues I'm used to addressing—but that doesn't mean I'm indisputably right. It only means that the lessons I pass on represent the best perspective I've arrived at so far, and I'm always learning, just as you are.

So let me acknowledge up front that for every principle I discuss, yes, you can probably think of an exception. So can I. As a teacher and literary editor, I've read more than a hundred thousand short stories in my time, plus enough novels to cover several library walls. I've seen countless literary experiments, many of which paid off, and many of which didn't. The points I'll propose here might be true only ninety-nine times out of a hundred, so please regard them with whatever degree of suspicion feels warranted. I wouldn't want to be the one to deny you the freedom to fall off the roof, or stick your fork in the wall outlet.

1

SOME PRINCIPLES OF CRAFT

Write What You Know, Write What You Don't

If you've ever come within spitting distance of a writing class, you've probably heard that you should write what you know. That's good advice, but only for those who understand it. *Write what you know* is probably the most misunderstood, misapplied piece of advice in the field. Taken to the improper extreme, it leaves little room for anything more than thinly veiled autobiography. After all, if the task is to write what we know, how can we stray from what has happened to us in our lives?

Obviously, we need to spread our wings more broadly than that. But where do we draw the line?

Over the years I've encountered writing teachers who have differed widely on this question. One told me that no writer should stray outside the perspective of his or her own economic level, as if our options should be defined by our respective tax brackets. One said no one should try to write characters outside his/her/their specific nationality or region of influence. One viewed it as taboo to create characters of any religion other than the sect in which one was raised. Several thought it impossible (or at least inappropriate) to write from the perspective of a gender or sexual orientation other than one's own.

I think many of those limitations are idiotic, and I suspect all sci-fi writers would agree with me. Some creative leaps do indeed require extreme sensitivity and research, but I would never tell you that any subject matter or point of view is off-limits.

There are those who would argue that we can't write truthfully about anything *foreign* to our lives, but I believe we are all, in some way or another, foreigners. We all know what it means to be a misfit, an outsider; we can all make the leap into writing the experience of *the other,* because we have all been *the other,* whether it was because of our race, our religion, our economic status, our weight, our height, our poor eyesight, or anything else that set us apart as a focus of taunts on the playground.

For that reason, I would not tell you that to write a Western you first need to drive a herd of longhorns up to Abilene. Nor would I say you can't write about the French Revolution unless you happen to be a three-hundred-year-old Frenchman.

In short, I do not subscribe to the notion that every central character should really be you, and the world you write about should be defined by the life you've actually lived.

Admittedly, some renowned authors have followed this narrow path, and if that's your natural inclination, I'm not going to tell you it's wrong. I just want you to realize that it's not the only way to go. Consider the words of Hemingway's mentor, Sherwood Anderson: *I think the whole glory of writing lies in the fact that it forces us out of ourselves and into the lives of others.* That's the team I play for.

The advice to write strictly from our own experience has often been attributed to Henry James, the great nineteenth-century novelist who emerged as the high-water mark of American Realism. But in fact James never believed any writer's realm should be so limited;

he asserted that experience came from everything, everywhere, and could be explored in infinite ways. James knew that *Write what you know* could be too easily misunderstood, so he offered a phrase to replace it: *Try to be one of the people on whom nothing is lost.*

In other words, from a mere glimpse we can extrapolate entire worlds. Yes, write from experience, but recognize that experience is far more vast than the literal daily activities you yourself engage in. The idea is not to narrow the scope of our writing, but to broaden it to include our collective world view, and to amplify that further through the expansive lens of imagination. Thus, we take our diverse fragments of experience and piece them together to form a new reality—one we haven't previously known.

Ultimately, we aren't writing about what it means to be a plumber, or a religious zealot, or an airline pilot, or a convict, or a king; we aren't writing about being homeless, or transexual, or differently abled, or fabulously wealthy, or terminally ill. Instead, we're writing about what it means to be *human,* and that will inevitably include thousands of traits and conditions and circumstances that might include any label we can think of. That's what empathy allows.

As I said, however, I don't want to shut down those who yearn to write fictionalized versions of their own lives, because it's possible to produce some fine work in that vein. Thomas Wolfe is a prime example. It's no secret that his first novel, *Look Homeward Angel,* was a scathing critique of the North Carolina town in which he grew up. He changed the name from Asheville to Altamont, but that didn't fool anyone, and the locals were outraged by his negative portrayal of their community. When his main character leaves to attend the state university, as Wolfe himself had done, he disguised the town of Chapel Hill by dubbing it Pulpit Hill, a charade that hardly seems worth the bother.

His second and third novels continued his own personal story. But it's important to remember that he was no lone gunman—he had great editors who removed hundreds of dull or digressive pages from his manuscripts and shaped his work into a readable form. Wolfe had many gifts as a writer, but because his source material was the story of his own life, he lacked the editorial distance to know what belonged *artistically* in that story and what didn't. That's the pitfall of autobiographical fiction.

That isn't to say you should keep yourself or your life experience out of your work. Far from it. Like Wolfe, or any other writer, for that matter, your life is your source. But don't think of your life as a story, think of it as a warehouse of raw materials. There are millions of items in that warehouse, and you can hand them out to whichever of your characters may need them. Utilize the world as you have experienced it, but don't limit yourself to story arcs mined from the nostalgia of your past. Write *from* yourself, not *about* yourself. Great fiction explores the hypothetical.

But maybe writing about yourself isn't the issue. Maybe what you want to do instead is bring the world a story based on a close friend or relative. After all, that's been done with spectacular success. Jack Kerouac famously made his friend, Neal Cassady, the model for Dean Moriarty in *On the Road*. What could go wrong in putting people you know in your fiction?

Well, plenty. And I'm not just talking about lawsuits.

When we write too close to home, we can develop a blindness toward our characters. Before we've written a single word about Uncle Harold, or Grandma Gussie, or our childhood friend Dave, we've already made up our minds about who they are. We know their looks, their styles, their attitudes, and their value systems.

Or at least we think we do. They exist in the black-and-white world of our pre-formed opinions. And because such characters already exist as fully developed people in our minds, our natural tendency is to leave them undeveloped on the page. For the writer, as soon as Grandma Gussie appears in the story sitting in her rocker on the front porch, she imbues the story with warm feelings stemming from personal memories. But the reader has no memories of Grandma Gussie. As far as the reader knows, she's an alcoholic, child-molesting, serial killer. The writer must therefore make a conscious effort to block out any personal feelings toward Grandma Gussie and portray her in fleshed-out detail, warts and all. That can be a challenge.

But I'm not about to tell anyone not to base any characters on real people. I only want you to know that, in some ways, it's far more difficult to write a plausible, multi-dimensional character if that character is based on a real live human being. Real people come to us complete in our imaginations, with no assembly required, and that can make us skimp on the details when we transfer that person to the page. Put a maroon sweater and a pair of Converse high-top sneakers on the character, and you can instantly see him as your best friend Curt from high school with all of Curt's manners, idiosyncrasies, and personality traits. But all the reader sees is a stranger in a maroon sweater and Converse high-tops.

On the other hand, when we invent from whole cloth, we tend to be more thorough, because the real world provides no mental shortcut for us as we conjure up the character. When a character is pure invention, we're on equal footing with the reader, knowing the character only from what's on the page. As a consequence, we tend to flesh out the character details more fully.

Pure invention, then, is the easier way to go. But that's not to say we have a license to write cavalierly or ignorantly about any unfamiliar culture or experience that strikes our fancy. As I've said, I believe that writers should be free to write about anything, but that comes with a caveat: the further away the subject matter is from our own personal experience, and the further away the character's identity is from our own, the greater the obligation for research.

Research, by the way, doesn't always mean looking up something on the internet. Sometimes just talking to the right person can provide all the specific insights your fiction might require. I once needed to write a scene in which a man got shot with an arrow. I wanted the injury to be serious but non-lethal, so I called my family doctor and asked him which organ was the most expendable. He told me we could do without a spleen, so that's where the arrow got lodged. If you need to set a scene during a Presbyterian church service, consult a minister. If you need technical information on hunting gear, visit a sporting goods store and talk to a knowledgeable sales clerk. People are always happy to share their expertise. So talk to plumbers, electricians, policemen, doctors, hunters, athletes, lumberjacks—whoever has the inside scoop on whatever world you're trying to create. They can provide you with the details to give your work a sense of authenticity.

Why is authenticity so important? Because no matter how engaging the characters and plot may be, readers won't go for the story unless they believe in the world in which it unfolds. It isn't good enough to base that world on what you've seen on television or in movies. If you want to set a scene in a courtroom, visit a courtroom to see how things are done. The same goes for a city council meeting, an arrest/booking procedure, a funeral, or whatever else you may want to portray realistically.

Apply this tactic to opposite-gender pieces, as well. Have a friend or two of the opposite sex read your manuscript and tell you where the voice rings false. If a character identifies in the LGBTQIA+ community and that's outside your own realm of experience, consult relevant members of that community. This kind of person-to-person research is one of the best ways to guard against reducing any character to a stereotype or a cliché.

The same burden holds true for any cultural, religious, or ethnic leap you choose to make in your writing. Write what you will, but face up to the responsibility of authenticity. Scrounge credibility from whatever unswept corner you may find. Rely on books, friends, memories, glimpses, and whatever else comes to hand.

And have no fear that life will not give you enough raw material to work with. We don't need to go out of our way to encounter life head on. The great Southern writer Flannery O'Connor felt that merely surviving childhood should give us all we need to know about life.

Ursula Le Guin's novel, *The Left Hand of Darkness,* is set on a distant planet peopled with characters who never know from one month to the next whether they will be male or female. Yet she makes her characters as plausibly human as any you'll find in your own neighborhood.

The lesson in this is an important one: violate any precondition of the world you wish, take any great leap your imagination can support, even into sci-fi or fantasy, but keep your characters aligned with a recognizable humanity. That's essential in keeping your readers sympathetic to your character's fate. This is true on any level, whether we're talking about Le Guin, O'Connor, Faulkner, Hemingway, or even Dr. Seuss. In *Horton Hears a Who,* we don't root for Horton because we like elephants, we root for him because his traits are our own. It isn't an enlarged Grinch heart that the Grinch gets at the end of *How the Grinch Stole Christmas,* it's a human one.

But how far can we take the notion of writing what we don't know? I'm in the camp of those who think writing is a voyage of discovery, that we're trying to understand what we're thinking, rather than parading the fine points of our education. Blind leaps on stony ground, that's my approach to writing fiction. It doesn't matter whether we're talking about mainstream literary fiction, or sci-fi, or fantasy, or westerns, or magic realism, or metafiction, or almost anything else. The process is the same, and the standards of the art remain the same.

Before a book can work, its parts have to work. A novel can't succeed unless its chapters do. A chapter can't succeed unless its paragraphs do. Paragraphs can't succeed unless sentences do. Sentences can't succeed unless the arrangements of individual word choices do.

To put it in story terms, no scene can work unless each micro-moment is made to be real. Everything has to start with the tiniest of snapshots, the micro-moment of captured reality.

I understand the appeal of outlining ahead of time. Having a template to work from can offer us a sense of security, especially if we're writing something as traditionally plot-based as a detective or mystery story. But even in those genres, creating an overly detailed outline can force story decisions to be based primarily on the needs of the plot. Each character then becomes a puppet in the service of the predetermined action line, which can result in seemingly unmotivated behavior. *Why did Bob throw the wrench through the window? Because the plot needed him to.* That breeds falseness in the story. Inner life—which allows us to care about your characters—gets sacrificed on the altar of timely action.

Any story that can be completely outlined ahead of time is unlikely to rise to the level of art. In such cases the writing itself becomes little more than an exercise in filling in the blanks. Those stories rarely contain spontaneous moments of surprise, unexpected epiphanies, or memorable discoveries. For the literate adult reader, there will be no lasting impact.

Whatever the genre, real literature arises only from proper attention to the molecular increments of writing, from split-seconds of spontaneous discoveries that add up to an extended truth.

Easier said than done.

How then do we arrive at these spontaneous discoveries that will keep our work moving forward? There are many ways, but the most common and useful may still be the "What if?" strategy. What if a young Danish prince found out that his uncle had murdered his father and married his mother? What if a young Englishman were raised by apes in the jungle? What if there were a school for wizards, and a special orphan got invited to attend? The *what ifs* are often how we get rolling on a story, but that approach can work on the micro level, as well.

What if a mother asks her son to drive to the store to buy apple juice? Ordinary event. But *what if* the son is fifteen and doesn't have a driver's license? Oh, that's a problem. But *what if* he feels obliged to go anyway? Why? Well, *what if* his mother is an alcoholic and wants the apple juice as a substitute for the gin in the cupboard? *What if* someone from social services is coming over that afternoon, and he has to make sure she stays sober? But *what if* he's terrified of driving because his father was killed in a car crash?

A thousand possible *what ifs* arise in every line of action, and these in turn require you to answer questions about what your character's responses might be. You'll have to think through the implications of every decision you make in a story, tracing out what the ramifications of each choice may be.

As you mull over these choices, these *what ifs,* think backwards as well as forwards. *What if* I change a pivotal detail from earlier in the story? How will that better serve where the story is now, or where it might be headed?

What we're talking about here is weaving threads into fabric. Think of a piece of silk—a fabric woven so tightly that even water will have a hard time seeping through. Yet the individual silk strand is incredibly thin. Create your stories in this manner; weave a web of experience so dense that it takes on the qualities of tightly woven fabric. Make each strand the product of a multitude of micro-decisions, micro-choices that you have proposed to yourself along the way.

◆ ◆ ◆

Let me be clear: the path I'm suggesting is the path of greatest resistance, the path most difficult to follow. It is the anti-formula. Write without knowing from one paragraph to the next what will follow. Focus only on the promises implied in the sentence you've just written, and think no further than what the next sentence should be. Make that second sentence an organic extension of the life of that first sentence. Then go to the third sentence, and wrestle with it until it fulfills the promise of the first two and carries their momentum forward toward a fourth sentence.

Invent story complications. Paint yourself into corners, burden your characters with obstacles, handicaps, weaknesses—don't give them many moments of emotional rest. Keep the tension alive from one micro-moment to the next, and be patient enough to fuse these lines into a seamless, silken reality. Working in this way, you can fully inhabit your characters in the present moment. Then just give them something to respond to—a thunderstorm, a gift, a slap, bad news, a stubbed toe, anything that will allow you to think through what a natural reaction might be, a reaction that will teach both you and your reader something new about the inner life of the character.

Then put another land mine in the character's life, and another, and another, an ongoing string of land mines, each one triggering a revelatory moment. They don't have to be gigantic melodramatic explosions, of course—sometimes only the tiniest of firecrackers might be called for, a little something that will disrupt the moment and, perhaps, cause a new thought, a new awareness, a new direction. Create such a journey of revelatory moments and you will have created a story for a reader to invest in.

In short, don't think you have to know the story before you can write it. Just keep moving forward along your string of complications until you see a potential ending to the character and story arcs. And never fear: potential endings litter the landscape, and you can find one any time you truly need to (more about that later). Meanwhile, see if you can build up some cruising speed. Concentrate not on where you're going, but on generating momentum in each present moment of the story. See how far it'll take you.

The key lies in trusting the unknown. Think of your fiction as a walk through the forest at night along a winding trail. Because there are so many twists and turns, your flashlight can never illuminate more than the ground immediately ahead of you. But that's all you need to stay on the path. Trust that the trail will take you through to the other side.

Granted, it can be a scary thing to embark on a huge writing project and not know exactly where you're going. All manner of self-doubt will plague you at every sentence. You'll worry that you're wasting precious time, you'll fear that nothing will work out. But like early mariners, you have to have faith that you're far more likely to reach an undiscovered landfall than to sail off the edge of the world. Allow yourself to be surprised—because if you surprise yourself, you'll stand a far better chance of surprising the reader.

The great challenge and joy of writing fiction is to make progress toward a place we've never known, a place in fact that won't exist in concrete form until the very moment we arrive there.

That place we don't know is Plato's ideal realm, the sanctuary of great art, where the story you're searching to write exists in its most perfect form. You'll never get near that place by following an outline. But you can come close to it by listening to the truth of your own experience.

2

BEGINNINGS

The First Step Off the Cliff Is the Most Dangerous

In the beginning, you probably had a parent or a teacher or maybe even a few classmates who read your work and applauded it. Few would venture very far down the writing road without some form of encouragement early in the journey. In all likelihood those early readers were dutiful cheerleaders, and you could count on them to keep trudging ahead through your work all the way to that final sentence you were so proud of. But now the paradigm has shifted. Sure, you're still writing for those you know, but you're also writing for strangers, and those strangers don't owe you a thing.

In fact, it's just the opposite: you owe them. It isn't their job to encourage you to keep writing, but it is your job to encourage them to keep reading. So the first rule for any writer has to be this: Never write with the expectation that anyone is required to finish reading what you've written. Obligation is simply not the reality in which a voluntary reader operates. There are just too many interesting things to do in the world for anyone to waste time on something boring, opaque, or clumsily made. As the late poet William Stafford was fond of reminding us, *The reader extends no credit.* Give a reader a reason to stop, and the reading will stop. It's that simple.

Of course, I'm not talking about what happened to so many of us in high school, or even in college. We were prisoners then, bound to finish whatever famous piece of literature showed up on the syllabus. In that context, we've all been forced to read thick books with slow, tedious openings—books the teachers urged us to appreciate because they were *classics.* Let me tell you now: don't use those books as your role models. There are many works of historical literary significance that go unread except inside a classroom, and deservedly so. Some writers became giants because their style altered the literary landscape, and we can still learn a great deal about writing from those pivotal figures. But that doesn't necessarily mean we'll find much pleasure or engagement in reading them today.

I happen to admire the complex prose of Henry James, but I also understand that his style of storytelling isn't going to attract many non-academic readers in modern society. In fact, James had stopped attracting readers even in his own lifetime, so much so that he continued to publish only through the charity of his friends. In 1912, Edith Wharton secretly paid Charles Scribner $8,000 to subsidize the publication of James's novel, *The Ivory Tower.* Yet James remains one of the great theoreticians of fiction writing and a staple of graduate seminars everywhere.

How can we explain this gap between the fame of the author and the apparent unreadability of his prose? It's nothing more than a matter of changing times. Literature is usually most potent in its own day, and as the world evolves, that power necessarily diminishes. We aren't the audience James was writing for. His heyday was in the late 1800s, when he led the way from literary Romanticism into Realism. In his own time, James was nothing less than a revolutionary writer. But his particular revolution is virtually irrelevant today, as dated as the monocles and buggy whips we might find among his pages.

True, some literature transcends its time period—Jane Austen comes to mind. But don't let the exceptions lead you too far astray. Imitating Jane Austin's prose style might not get you very far as a contemporary writer, for the simple reason that her voice is not your voice. She was a product of her own time; you are a product of yours. And I'm sorry to break the news, but your challenges as a writer are a little more complicated than the ones Jane Austin faced.

Imagine, for example, that you lived six thousand years ago and invented the game of checkers. Your mud hut would be the most popular hangout in the valley. Everyone would want to play your new game. But try bringing your checkerboard into one of today's gaming arcades. You won't draw much interest because checkers can't compete with the dynamics of modern video games. When the novel first came on the scene, those writers were cave-dwellers inventing checkers in that they had little competition for their audience's attention. Comparatively fewer books were being published, for one thing, and since the novel was a new form—hence the name—no one knew quite what to expect from it. In those early days, even a bad novel could still qualify as one of the best ever written.

Perhaps more importantly, there weren't that many alternative forms of entertainment for the solitary participant. One could embroider, or garden, or take up a musical instrument, or paint watercolors, but that was about it. I suppose after dark one could stare at the stars, but that's not much of a page-turner.

Today's writers, on the other hand, are writing for a culture numbed by a relentless barrage of options, a culture of short attention spans, of immediate gratification. Both writer and reader have been bombarded with more storytelling experience than any generation in world history. Never has there been so jaded an audience as the one you must now write for.

So if you want to be read, your first job is to convince

the reader that your piece of fiction is the most interesting activity available. That convincing has to happen without delay, because your potential reader has a thousand other options. For that simple reason, the most important sentence in any work of fiction is the first.

Hemingway had famously lofty beliefs about opening sentences, believing that the first sentence should somehow contain the entire story. I like that notion—not that the sentence should literally sum up the narrative, but that it should contain all the pent-up power of the story, like a stick of dynamite with a freshly lit fuse.

But whatever anyone's view may be of what the opening sentence should or should not contain, that sentence will always have one essential job: to make the reader read the second sentence. The second has to make us read the third, and the third has to make us read the fourth. Any stumble that breaks the chain—releasing the reader from the text or undercutting faith in the author—can be disastrous to the fiction. The earlier the stumble, the more likely it is to cause a destructive break. And in my nearly fifty years of teaching and my twenty-five years of editing literary journals, I've found story openings to be where most inexperienced writers make their fatal mistakes.

I once tried an experiment at a literary magazine I was editing. I grabbed a few dozen unread fiction submissions and gave them to my board of twenty readers. I asked half of them to read the manuscripts in their entirety, and the other half to read just the opening page. In selecting which manuscripts to recommend, each group came to the same editorial conclusions, identifying the same few manuscripts as publishable. Sometime afterwards, I mentioned this experiment to poet and editor Carolyn Kizer, and she told me she had once done the same thing at a magazine she was editing, with the same results. From the editorial perspective, then, I'd say opening paragraphs are a pretty good weathervane for determining whether a story is headed toward publication or the rejection pile. That's an important thing for writers to know.

At the majority of journals, magazines, and publishing houses, there will be an editorial chain of command, and your manuscript will have to survive a series of trained readers to make it all the way to publication. A bad response from any intern or assistant editor along the way will land you in the rejection pile, along with 98% of the other writers trying to get published. I hope this doesn't come as a shocking revelation, but if a manuscript falters at the beginning, most editors will stop reading after a paragraph or two. The idea that you can win them back later with some exciting and brilliant twist on page twelve is nothing short of delusional, because they won't make it that far.

That doesn't mean editors don't take their work seriously. On the contrary, editors like nothing better than to discover great manuscripts, but because they do take their work seriously, they have to be efficient in working through the mountainous pile of submissions covering their desktops. They can't afford to waste time slogging through weak material that has already done itself in on the opening page. Thanks to the wild proliferation of creative writing programs over the past two generations, a mid-level magazine might easily receive, say, two thousand manuscripts a year, out of which it can publish only twenty. The knee-jerk rejection is a practical necessity.

That doesn't mean the editors are your enemy, no matter what your bruised ego would have you believe. Editors will always approach your manuscript with a sense of hope; they will always root for it to succeed. But they have to be cut-throat in their decision making, because other manuscripts are waiting.

When I was in graduate school, Kurt Vonnegut came in for a visit to the writing program. He told us a lot of good things about the craft of writing, but the most important was his answer to a simple generic question.

Someone in the room asked him if he had any advice to help would-be writers. "Sure," he said. "Cut the first six pages."

That line got a laugh at the time. But year after year I've experienced the wisdom of what he was telling us. Like many other lessons I've encountered along the way, it took me a while to understand the insight Vonnegut was offering, but it finally sank in. His advice was sound, and for several reasons.

The first is that it's our natural tendency to try too hard at the beginning. We want to impress the reader with our writing ability, so we strain to show off. We push our language a little too far, resulting in artificially inflated prose.

The second reason we might foul up our openings is our failure to trust the reader. We front-load too much exposition—material that is often irrelevant or would eventually become self-evident if we just got on with the story. Instead, we labor over constructing a long runway before ever getting the story off the ground. If we're telling a joke, we already know to start with *A guy walks into a bar. . .* without describing the route he took to get there. We should apply that instinct to our fiction.

A third reason (though related to the second) for inefficient story openings has to do with our educational system itself. From the time we were in grade school, we were taught to write in a particular structure: introduction, body, and conclusion. That academic structure is our default mechanism, and we'll automatically fall into it unless we consciously avoid it. And we should avoid it, because stories, on the whole, do not require introductions or conclusions. An introduction stalls the forward movement, and an overt conclusion is condescending, since it assumes the reader didn't understand the story. Leave introductions to the editors and conclusions to the critics. Let the writer stick with writing just the body. Open with the story, not with an introduction to the story.

Has Vonnegut's six-page rule held true? Not universally, of course. But in my editing experience, I can say that the majority of rejected manuscripts had extraneous material up front that should have been cut from the manuscript. And countless times, in reading a piece of student work, I've made a notation somewhere near the bottom of page six: *Story starts here.*

Sometimes writers can get away with an introduction—as I've said, there are exceptions to virtually every principle of good storytelling. Edgar Allen Poe's "The Telltale Heart" opens with a brief introductory paragraph before moving on to the story. But Poe handled the introduction in such a way as to make it a crucial part of the story:

> True, nervous, very very dreadfully nervous I had been and am, but why will you say that I am mad? The disease had sharpened my senses, not destroyed, not dulled them. Above all was my sense of hearing acute. I heard all the things in heaven and earth. I heard many things in hell. How then am I mad? Harken, and observe how calmly, how carefully I can tell you the whole story.

That introduction accomplishes a lot that the story needs. It isn't merely expository, it's revelatory, setting both tone and mood. It also establishes the insanity of the narrator, and it raises questions about what exactly this nutjob has been up to. Notice that Poe kept the introduction short—one pithy paragraph—so the reader is less likely to lose patience.

Then the second paragraph, which starts the story proper, offers an immediate hook: "I was never kinder to the old man than during the whole week before I killed him." So in this one-two set-up we have a brief introduction followed by a solid story opening, and they work together to draw the reader forward into the tale. Arguably, the story would still work just fine without the introduction, but in this case I'm willing to give the writer some slack. It's Poe, after all. But the key point is this: even with the introduction in place, Poe never gives us time to lose patience. We're plunged immediately into a dynamic situation fraught with tension.

Let's not forget that Poe was a well-read scholar, quite familiar with theories of storytelling structure. Classical Greek and Roman works were well within his purview, so it's no coincidence that, in terms of structure, he shared Aristotle's position about beginnings. Aristotle advocated the *in media res* approach, the one that plunges us immediately into the action. His advice was to start the story as far along the line of action as possible and to fill us in on relevant backstory as the plot moves forward.

Aristotle would have been a severe editor, by the way. He believed that stories should be so tightly constructed that not a single line could be removed without destroying the tale's coherence. Each line had to be part of an unbroken chain of cause and effect. Stalling the action with an academic introduction would thus be anathema; such introductions tend to announce chain reactions without actually starting them. But think of a line of falling dominoes; remove any single domino and the chain reaction will stop.

If you think starting a story off on the right foot is a good idea, but you don't have a clear notion of how to do that, here are four tactics I've encountered that work pretty well as opening gambits:

The unlikely statement
The case of strange behavior
The engaging voice
The tension-filled situation

So, let's look at these tactics in greater detail.

◆ ◆ ◆

The unlikely statement is an easy way to raise questions for the reader. If you say something that seems unlikely to be true, the reader can't resist sticking around to find out just what the heck you're talking about.

Rick Bass begins his story "Mississippi" with the line, "As you know, there are no more Coca-Colas in Mississippi." Who could resist reading a little further to find out what's going on?

Ditto for Aimee Bender's story, "The Healer," which opens with "There were two mutant girls in the town: one had a hand made of fire and the other had a hand made of ice."

Mark Twain began his book, *Captain Stormfield's Visit to Heaven,* with this line: "Well, when I had been dead for about thirty years, I begun to get a little anxious."

And as long as we're visiting the nineteenth century, let's not overlook Charles Dickens: "It was the best of times, it was the worst of times." The statement is enigmatic and self-contradictory—and it encourages us to keep going.

Of course, the obligation of a sentence like any of these is to go on and explain the way in which the statement is true. Crazy, random claims might get the reader to the second sentence, but if you're just flinging odd statements around to attract attention, you'll lose your reader in a hurry. Readers love exploring the seemingly inexplicable, but they don't warm to pointless chaos.

Obviously, the tactic might come more naturally when one is writing in a fantastical vein. Exploring magical reversals of reality might, at first glance, seem more interesting than reading about the world of Ordinary Joe who works the counter at the Chevron station.

The case of strange behavior can involve anybody, including Ordinary Joe, who might have all kinds of extraordinary things going on in his life. Tell us that an hour before Ordinary Joe got married he sold his comic book collection so he could rent John Dillinger's fedora to wear for the ceremony, and we'll probably wonder what kind of person would do a thing like that, and why. And if we wonder about something, we'll tend to keep reading.

Consider the great opening line of David Jauss's story, "Torque," which introduces us to an offbeat Ordinary Joe—or in this case, Ordinary Larry:

> The day after his wife left him, taking their three-year-old son with her, Larry Watkins took out his circular saw, attached the metal-cutting blade, and carefully sawed his 1974 Cadillac Fleetwood in half.

As this opening demonstrates, Ordinary Larry isn't so ordinary after all. That's an opening sentence that will keep us moving forward.

The engaging voice is a little trickier, especially in third-person narration, because it requires the immediate establishing of personality.

The voice of the teenager-with-attitude is often a crowd pleaser—Holden Caulfield in Salinger's *The Catcher in the Rye,* comes to mind, as well as Huckleberry Finn as he recounts his own adventures. Teen voices are often rooted in a rejection of the status quo, and a negative or snarky world view can certainly be entertaining—or even chilling. Kaye Gibbons opens her novel *Ellen Foster* with a preteen girl thinking of ways to kill her father.

The voice also might simply deviate from the norm, which is the tactic James Joyce employs in the first line of *A Portrait of the Artist as a Young Man:*

> Once upon a time and a very good time it was there was a moocow coming down

> along the road and this moocow that was coming down along the road met a nicens little boy named baby tuckoo.

Sometimes the engaging voice is comically quirky, as we find in Mark Twain's metafictional opening of *The American Claimant:*

> No weather will be found in this book. This is an attempt to pull a book through without weather. It being the first attempt of the kind in fictitious literature, it may prove a failure, but it seemed worth the while of some dare-devil person to try it, and the author was just in the mood.

There's no story here yet, just an engaging voice, seeking to appeal to our playful side.

The tension-filled situation can be a strong way to open any story. This is one of the more common approaches—because it works.

Tell us that Ordinary Josephine robbed a liquor store an hour before she got married so she could pay for the honeymoon, and we'll probably stick around to see just how disastrous these circumstances will become.

Tell us that Ordinary Joe had just reached the top of the ladder when he felt the first faint tremor of the earthquake, and we'll probably stick around to see if he took the fall.

One of the better examples of this tactic that I've come across is the opening sentence of Leslie Mitchell's *Spartacus:*

> When Kleon heard the news from Capua, he rose early one morning, being a *literatus* and unchained, crept to his master's room, stabbed him in the throat, mutilated that

> master's body even as his own had been mutilated, and so fled from Rome with a stained dagger in his sleeve and a copy of *The Republic* of Plato hidden in his breast.

Talk about a tension-filled situation.

I'm not suggesting that your openings always have to introduce some weird voice, or melodramatic predicament, or general strangeness, or seeming-impossibility. Those openings certainly ensnare the reader, but we needn't start every story with a plane crash, or some pending act of violence, or a magical elf speaking in tongues. The tension you introduce doesn't have to be life-threatening, or even life-altering, but any opening with no tension at all or no question raised for the reader is doomed to be a three-legged horse in the Derby.

Admittedly there are more ways to open a story successfully beyond the four cornerstones I'm mentioned here. These four might be among the most reliable, but there are other routes to winning over the reader. Literary style, for example. A lyrical leap or an enigmatic metaphor can sometimes engage a reader's attention as effectively as a copperhead in the cookie jar.

But what do I mean by style? What do I mean by a lyrical leap? Well, here's an example from Thomas Wolfe's *Look Homeward Angel*:

> Which of us has known his brother? Which of us has looked into his father's heart? Which of us has not remained forever prison-pent? Which of us is not forever a stranger and alone?
>
> O waste of lost, in the hot mazes, lost, among bright stars on this weary, unbright cinder, lost! Remembering speechlessly we seek the great forgotten language, the lost lane-end into heaven, a stone, a leaf, an

unfound door. Where? When?
O lost, and by the wind grieved, ghost,
come back again.

That's more than just an everyday passage of prose, it's poetry—and it's difficult not to be impressed by it.

But that lovely sequence wasn't the opening of his novel, it was embedded deep in the story after everything else got well under way. Any writer might suddenly enter into a lyrical passage of unforced poeticism, but such magical leaps are usually something that the writer has been building toward—often unconsciously. Successful lyrical openings are few and far between, because trying to dazzle a reader with lofty poeticism right out of the gate carries risks. The reader might think that you're trying too hard, or that you're being pretentious. Or they might think the entire book will be like that and be hesitant to wade through it.

When lyricism works, it can be quite memorable, so I wouldn't discourage you from trying it. But be aware that it's a difficult approach to pull off. Lyricism is the literary equivalent of a circus high-wire act, and most of us are still in the dusty ring down below, struggling to emerge from the clown car.

So there you have it: four pragmatic tactics for starting a story, plus one iffy bonus option for the poets or the over-confident.

There are other ways to open a story, of course—427 in all—though I'll leave it to you to ferret those out. But notice that these four—and the rest—have one thing in common: they give the reader a reason to keep reading, usually through the raising of a question.

Now take a look at your own work and see if your opening line does that. Not your tenth line, or your fifth, but your first. If that first line doesn't give the reader an identifiable reason to move forward through the text, then maybe you haven't found the right point of entry for your story.

◆ ◆ ◆

But don't think you're in the clear after your brilliant, engaging opening line. In a sense, you have to start over with each new paragraph, each new page, each new chapter. Chapter breaks for the novelists present a particular challenge, because chapter breaks are also reader breaks. Rarely are books read in one sitting, so you have to assume the reader has put the book down at some point and has now picked it up to become reengaged with the material. Since chapter breaks make logical stopping points, each new chapter should begin with some kind of hook to draw the reader back into the story.

I'd suggest starting each new chapter the way you might start a short story—in the middle of the action, in a situation that will ensnare the reader quickly. The further into the book you get, the easier the reengagement process will become, because the reader will, to some extent, have been won over already. But never assume that you've got the reader captive and can just set the story on cruise control until the end. Plenty of readers fail to finish books. There are some people who don't much like reading at all. I would encourage you to write with those nonreaders in mind. If you can write a piece that even a nonreader can't put down, you've really got something.

That's what we all have to do with our prose: write stories that refuse to let go. Why? Because once we do let go of the reader, we may not get a second chance. Take the reader for granted, and soon you'll have no reader. Remember that the reader is constantly being called away from your book by the world's other diversions and obligations. There are movies to watch, and television shows to follow, and music to listen to, and video games to play, and social-network friends to catch up with. There's also eating and sleeping and bowling and Ping-Pong and dating and gardening and knitting and just about anything else you can imagine. That's the competition—not to mention other books that may be more engaging than yours—and the competition is relentless. That's why we can't afford to botch our beginnings.

I've already mentioned that writing a story can be like following a path through a forest at night. But of course the first step is to discover where the path begins, and that in itself can be difficult. We may have to chop through a lot of undergrowth and brambles, but sooner or later, there it is, that miraculous clearing in the trees, and we can begin to find our direction.

That's often the case with me, anyway—and I don't think I'm unusual in that regard. I've never heard of any writer who routinely had an easy time with story openings. Ernest Hemingway wrote a wonderful first novel—*The Sun Also Rises*—or rather, he eventually wrote a wonderful first novel of that title. The beginning gave him all kinds of trouble, and so he sent a draft of it to his friend, F. Scott Fitzgerald. Fitzgerald was brutal in his critique, and at one point called the opening *mere horseshit.* Hemingway took the criticism to heart. In revision, he went even further than Vonnegut might have suggested: rather than cutting the first six pages, he cut the first fifteen.

Certainly we've all come across examples of novels or stories we eventually came to love even though they started slowly. Usually, those turn out to be books by authors of whom we're already fans, which means we may be more inclined to grant them the benefit of the doubt. But remember that a slow opening is always a risk, and the longer you delay setting the hook, the greater the chance the reader will slip away from you and go back to surfing the internet for videos of kittens getting stuck in cookie jars.

CHARACTER

Mr. Potato Head vs. Freud

You probably remember Mr. Potato Head—that bulbous blob of plastic that brightened your childhood with its many attachable accessories: lips, eyes, eyebrows, a mustache, glasses, even a pipe (though why a potato would smoke a pipe was never made clear). These various parts could be stuck on the body to create an identity for the potato. Then the parts could be swapped out for others to create a change in personality. Mr. Potato Head was one of the early devices that showed us how to create characters through external means. There were others, of course. For example, the only difference between Malibu Barbie and Brain Surgeon Barbie is the outfit she wears. The external difference is what defines the character.

But then we graduated from play-school and went to real school, where they introduced us to Freud. That's when we learned about all the gooey stuff inside—the sticky globs of resentment we hold toward our parents, the icy bitterness we harbor for being bossed around by authority figures, the leaden guilt we carry for failing those we love, the insecurities, the heartaches, the disappointments, the secret rage we nurture against perceived injustices, the paralyzing fear of being seen for who we are, or being overlooked entirely, or being bullied, or being embarrassed, or being disillusioned, or being dead. The interior landscape is more vast than the external, just as the inner workings of a clock will always be more complex than whatever happens on its face.

I use the clock metaphor for a reason. It's mechanical, rather than organic, and though, in many ways, characters can be both mechanically constructed and organically grown, the mechanical is a more accessible starting point.

One of the great theorists of modern acting technique was the Russian theatrical director Constantin Stanislavsky. Though he was primarily concerned with performance art, Stanislavsky has a lot to teach writers about creating characters. He was famous for urging his actors to *live* the part, rather than *act* it. He trained his actors to summon up real emotion rather than to put on a false potato face.

Yet when Stanislavsky wrote a book about the process, he called it *Building a Character.* Not growing a character, but building one. Spontaneity could be good, but for consistency and clarity, he believed, the actor should always be in control, should always pick and choose what actions, gestures, and attitudes were most appropriate for any given character at any particular time. Stanislavsky was the one to require actors to invent an extensive subtext for the characters they portrayed. He was convinced that knowing the character's life off-stage would enhance the performance on-stage, giving it more depth. He believed that every action—indeed every thought—had to stem from real motivation, and the key to motivation lay in the character's background from which identity had been formed.

Those of us on the writing side of the creative fence are indebted to Stanislavsky for pioneering the concept of subtext—though we might prefer terms like *inner life* and *backstory*. It's no coincidence that Anton Chekhov, the father of the modern character-based short story, was brought to prominence by Stanislavsky, who, as Director of the Moscow Art Theatre, introduced many of Chekhov's greatest plays to the world.

Subtext is the source of a character's motivation, and motivation comes from the life lived both on and off the page. Every action, every thought, every line of dialogue must be an extension of who the character is at that precise moment. And because people are not automatons, we cannot assume a universal response to the same stimuli. Our responsibility as writers is to understand why one character might react to a slap with anger while another might react with tears, or confusion, or shock, or even laughter. The characters we create must respond to all things as individuals, not as types; they must act or react according to the context of what time and circumstance have caused them to be. Once we establish the subtext of a character, the reader can then find revelatory intent in even the most trivial or mundane exchange or interaction.

Characters occasionally dwell in the extremes, but for the most part they reside in the realm of everyday subtleties. Instead of breaking into crescendos of *I love you!* or *I hate you!* at every bend in the road, realistic characters are far more likely to say *Pass the salt.* But if the character is properly drawn, the reader will know that beneath a line like *Pass the salt* there could be shadings of value that give even so simple a line myriad possibilities of meaning—love, hate, fear, insecurity, arrogance, or anything else supported by the character's precise state of emotional and psychological balance in the world.

Once depth of character has been established through the development of subtext, the mundane suddenly becomes charged with tension and significance. Every action and word acquires weight. We can then advance beyond the denotative level to the connotative; from the emptiness of mere shadow-play to the consequential interactions that reveal inner life, where meaning resides.

Subtext gives characters internal consistency. Only by laying this proper groundwork of characterization can we hope to approach the verisimilitude necessary to capture and convey the full spectrum of the human experience.

The notion that identity is shaped by subtext leads us back to Freud, with whom Stanislavsky can be seen as philosophically aligned. Both considered personality to be the product of past experience. In today's terminology, we would say they were both Scientific Determinists. For that matter, so is Mr. Potato Head, who is the product of the features he's been stuck with.

So whether we're talking about the external or the internal, Mr. Potato Head or Freud, we're talking about character as an artificially constructed self, a collection of conscious choices on the part of the writer.

But surely Mr. Potato Head is a superficial triviality. Surely his contributions can't compare to Freud's side of the equation, where dredged-up demons of a warped psyche can ruin a character's life. Surely external details are little more than window dressing when it comes to building a character, and Hamlet's anguish over his murdered father carries infinitely more weight than Mr. Potato Head's mustache.

Well, not necessarily.

Hulga, in Flannery O'Connor's story, "Good Country People," is defined by the fact that she has an artificial leg. In Hulga's case, most of her character derives from that one fact.

Her attitude of false superiority, her academic drive, her snide interactions with others, even her vulnerability to being duped by a traveling bible salesman who lures her to a hayloft for romance and promptly steals her leg—all of these traits stem psychologically from that one external character detail: her physical difference and how she copes with it. That's a rich use of the Mr. Potato Head approach as a starting point. The external detail comes first and triggers everything internal that follows from it.

That same character arc is true of Ahab, by the way, who lost his leg to Moby Dick and allowed that physical loss to fuel the obsession that defined everything else about him from that moment on.

But not all physical traits take us on such all-encompassing journeys of characterization. When we were young and we read about Curious George and his friend, the Man in the Yellow Hat, all we ever really learned about them as characters was that George was curious and that his friend wore a yellow hat. That kind of limitation can work fine for a children's story, but making the leap to literary fiction would require more than just piling on more external details. The story of Curious Flea-Infested George, for example, would probably not take us to any greater depths of the monkey's psyche.

But I've seen many student writers attempt to do just that. They provide a veritable anatomy text of physical description without ever giving any of it any relevance or depth. Why do we need to know the color of a character's eyes? So they're brown—so what? Unless there's a psychological reason for it to matter, why tell us? So what if a male character is five-foot-eleven? What does it matter? Three-foot-eleven would matter, and so would six-foot-eleven, because then height would become an issue with the way the character interacts with the world. But once you start specifying that your male protagonist is six feet tall with wavy black hair, rippling biceps, and piercing blue eyes, we'll think we're reading a cheesy dime-store romance novel.

J.D. Salinger gives us only the barest handful of physical details about Holden Caulfield, but that's not a knock against *The Catcher in the Rye*. In Henry James's day, before the world had such things as television or film, a writer might impress a reader with an overload of description. Literary Realism, as I've mentioned, was a mimetic art form, and readers of the time might appreciate a writer's providing a three-page account of someone pouring a cup of tea. But we're a more savvy and sophisticated readership than what Henry James was writing for, in the sense that our concept of visual projection is far more advanced. We don't need every gap filled in for us.

Now, yes, it's important for us to get a full external description of Jay Gatsby and all his trappings because we need to understand the superficial and false identity in which he has cloaked himself to fit in with the wealthy aristocracy. Gatsby is a classic Mr. Potato Head, because the totality of his physical appearance is a legitimate expression of character. His Mr. Potato Head self is at war with his Freudian self, so there's actual story tension in the multitude of fancy shirts he pulls from his closet in a pathetic attempt to prove his worth to Daisy.

But Gatsby aside, description for description's sake is often a dead end that stalls the momentum of a story. Sure, if a character is bald or freckled or hairy or underweight and he or she feels self-conscious about it, then by all means include the detail. Any external trait that connects with the inner life of the character is legitimate. But if neither the character nor anybody else in the story is affected by the trait, the reader might not need to be told about it.

Of course, sometimes we use minor characters who appear only briefly and who may best be identified through the shorthand of some striking feature or trait. *Mary noticed the skeletal-looking beatnik in the black-beret lurking at the back of the coffee shop.* Maybe this fellow is just passing through the story and we'll never know anything more about him, or maybe he'll turn out to be important. But at this particular moment, we don't need a full inventory of his wardrobe, we need only to know what caught Mary's eye.

The exception would be if Mary has been searching for this character throughout the story—a long-lost cousin or brother or lover, someone for whom she would have a psychological reason to absorb more visual details. Maybe the man is the father she never met, and she has always wondered what color his eyes were; then eye color becomes relevant. Maybe seeing his shabby clothes and stubble of a beard makes her worry about his health or financial situation; then clothing and grooming become relevant. Let the degree of description fit the relative psychological significance of the character's entry into the story. Show us only as much of the outside as is relevant.

Granted, for the most part, when we think of character in literary fiction (and by literary fiction I mean character-based works in all the genres), we usually think of Freud's side of the toolbox. That's natural. I would argue that the inner life is not only what matters most to character but to story itself. The best storytelling deals with experiences, not events. Events are external, whereas experiences are about what develops in the people to whom the events have happened. How the world intrudes upon and reshapes our inner lives, that's what good literary fiction is about; the shift in the inner landscape.

But how do we go about constructing that landscape? How do we build a character's Freudian insides? Well, the same way we would with Mr. Potato Head. We make choices and apply them to the character. We decide about the details of inner life and backstory.

For example, suppose you're writing a story about a woman who works as a receptionist in a doctors' office. A new doctor joins the practice, and he develops an interest in our protagonist, whom he finds attractive. Let's say he's a perfectly fine fellow who owns a pair of golden retrievers and has a house on the beach. If we stop there in our character development all we have are the makings of a lame office-romance story, smooth sailing all the way. But that's where backstory comes in. Let's say the receptionist's father abandoned her when she was five, leaving her mistrustful of love relationships. Say she was mauled by a Doberman when she was eleven, leaving her uneasy around big dogs. On top of all that, she witnessed her cousin drown at the beach one summer, so she has an aversion to the shore. She didn't have the money to go to college, so she feels insecure around highly educated professional people. Consequently, even though she works for doctors she feels paralyzed around them in social situations. And to make things even more of an uphill battle for our receptionist and her aspiring beau, maybe we even decide that ten years ago she was assaulted on prom night by someone who bears an unfortunate resemblance to the new doctor, and now every time he smiles at her, she flashes back to that long-ago moment of horror.

These are the seeds of conflict. The situation offers her a chance at a happy life, but her previous experience works against it. Goals are set at cross-purposes, not only between our two main characters but within the receptionist herself, who, in spite of all her baggage, is indeed attracted to the doctor. Now the characters have obstacles to overcome, inner demons to cope with, and this moves us from a run-of-the-mill romance novel into something more complex, something possibly more literary. As the characters become fleshed out in this way, in terms of their respective subtexts and backstories, the less predictable they'll become.

That may sound counterintuitive. One could reasonably assume that the more we know about a character, the more predictable that character might become. But in fact the more you flesh out a character, the more human a character becomes. The more human a character becomes, the more variables come into play. More variables means less predictability.

We all experience conflicting pressures every day, and so should our characters. We want to do one thing but feel we ought to do another. From day to day, who knows which path we'll choose? What is it in the real world that will one night make a normally good kid sneak out his bedroom window at midnight and steal a car to go joyriding? Maybe he'll do it only once in his entire life, but something on that one night made him deviate from the norm. In fiction we're always looking for those moments of pressure in which the character deviates from the normal routine, the day on which the perfect combination of present circumstance and prior history create a volatile new mix, and something inside changes forever.

A great example of a writer who builds characters psychologically from the ground up is Anne Tyler, particularly in her novel, *Dinner at the Homesick Restaurant.* The three siblings in that book are scarred from their shared childhood, and as we watch them move through their separate adult lives, we understand the deep-seated psychological motivations underlying every action they take, even though each follows a different behavioral path. Nothing they do is predictable, but everything they do is understandable because we know their backstories.

An important point to remember is that as you build your characters, you won't do it all at once. Part of the process of writing a story is discovering who the characters are, and that means adding to the backstory as you move forward. Sometimes it even means changing backstory to fit the ever-shifting needs of the narrative. In each draft, find ways to apply more pressure to your characters. As the poet A.R. Ammons once advised aspiring writers, "Pile entanglements on." I've always found that advice useful, especially in fiction.

Another important fact to remember is that the character is not you. Most of the building blocks inevitably come from you, from your experience with the world, but the character may react differently to a situation in which you once found yourself. That's because the character doesn't possess the totality of your experience to shape his or her reactions. Your job in assembling the character is to pick and choose from your storehouse of experiences and give the character only those parts of yourself that the character needs.

Though it may again seem counterintuitive, borrowing a character from real life can present more pitfalls than building one on your own, because, as I've mentioned before, you can easily lose your editorial distance. Editorial distance is crucial; it's the emotional or psychological separation from the work that gives you a proper critical perspective. Too much real-world closeness to a character can hamper your imaginative thoroughness. While you might view the character as fully alive, the reader might see only a rudimentary sketch, a cardboard cutout or stereotype.

Then, too, we might feel a natural reluctance to assign negative traits to characters based on people we know. That's a problem, because well-behaved people seldom make for good fiction. If you balk at showing us the ugly flaws of a character, or at telling lies about the real people you're substituting for characters, your story is likely to run aground.

Fiction is about telling lies to get at a greater truth, and if we try to be too respectful of the real people behind the story, we've saddled ourselves with a burden that has nothing to do with art. The real world and the people in it should be a springboard, not a straight-jacket. We need to guard against writing characters who are merely testimonials to those we love—or writing hatchet jobs about people we dislike. In either case we'll end up with stick-figure saints and villains. Characters of such limited dimensions can't hold a reader's interest for long.

So if you want to put real people into your fiction, be aware of the pitfalls. The writer's first allegiance is to the art, and not to those friends and family being recycled as characters.

Original invention is usually the more productive way to go. Build a new character from the ground up and you'll automatically have a head start on bringing life to the page, because you'll begin with the same editorial distance as a reader, getting to know the character only as it reveals itself through the story.

So build your characters from scratch, using the fragments of your own experience as the building blocks. That may sound limiting, since the number of run-ins you've had with the world is necessarily finite. But imagine your life experience as a deck of cards, with every hand you might deal from it a different character. The number of possible hands is astronomical, though they all come from the same limited deck.

Now, up to this point, everything I've suggested about constructing character has been mechanical. Whether approaching the task as Mr. Potato Head or as Freud, we're still consciously choosing which puzzle pieces of physicality and personality will fit into the frame. But I don't want to ignore the subconscious side of creation. We've probably all heard claims of characters unexpectedly taking over a story. Maybe that's happened to you. Lightning does strike. Not often, but if it happens, go with it. If you somehow plug into the rhythms of a particular voice, let yourself gush for as long as the gush will last.

Of course, that's when we may really be crossing into Freud's territory, or even Carl Jung's. Maybe that thing we're tapping into is a deeper level of the self, as Freud might contend, or maybe we're tapping into something larger, a collective unconscious, as Jung would say, where all archetypes of personality reside. Either way, it can be a good thing for the writer, particularly in a first-person narrative, where idiosyncrasies of voice might matter more than a carefully crafted prose style.

But even the purest gush will probably need revision. Spontaneous expression is not necessarily best expression, no matter the inspiration behind it. The language may still be raw. When oil is pumped from the ground it's pure oil, but it's still called *crude* and needs to be refined. Let yourself be self-indulgent in that first gushing draft, if that's a way you're comfortable working. Trust your instincts, which are always right on some level or another, and give voice to whatever seems true, honest, and natural. But then go back and shape the character and the character's language. Weed out inconsistencies that might damage credibility. Heighten elements that took a step in the right direction but didn't go far enough. Pull back on those moments that might be a little over the top. Search for the best way to phrase everything. Edit. Literary art is not an accidental process.

Yes, there are such things as found poems, and sometimes in prose we can enter into a lyrical leap that works without our having to think twice about it. But no literary career, or even a single book, can be built upon a calculated stream of lightning strikes. When it comes to building a character, we need to start with craft and hope the lightning strike will come, transforming the work into something greater than craft alone could ever account for. If we skip the step of craft—the conscious application of the tools we have at our disposal—we'll rarely if ever achieve art.

Character is the key to a reader's level of engagement in a story. Car chases and shoot-outs are of limited interest, except insofar as they involve people we care about. What happens on the surface—the sequence of events—matters only if the reader has an emotional or intellectual investment in the characters to whom the events are happening.

To accomplish that, we have to create more than a puppet. Every thought, gesture, and action should arise naturally from the identity of the character—from the traits that define who the character is.

One of the best ways to define any character is through desires. A round, dynamic character needs a goal to move toward, an internal or external condition in need of change. There's a practical reason for this: static characters who want nothing can't hold a reader's attention for very long. Virtually every memorable character in literature has something at stake emotionally, psychologically, or physically.

One strength I admire in the work of Flannery O'Connor is the absence of flat, static characters. Stanislavsky claimed there were no small parts, only small actors, and O'Connor seems to agree. Even her bit players get the full spotlight for the moment they are on stage, as if suddenly they've become the most important character in the story. Too often we can be tempted to place characters in our work merely as sounding boards or straight men for the main character. These stock figures ask the right questions and make the right observations at just the right times, but they aren't people, they're functionaries. O'Connor, however, makes each character a person, not a plot device. In the overall story, these minor characters might be of secondary or tertiary importance, but for as long as they're on the page, they take a backseat to nobody. That tactic enriches virtually every scene she writes.

Ultimately, in building characters there is no universally right or wrong approach. Just about anything can be made to work at least once. We're in the age of metafiction, experimentalism, magical realism, postmodernism, and who knows what other nontraditional avenues of storytelling, some of which define themselves specifically by the rules they choose to violate. Stories have been written in the form of tweets, PowerPoint presentations, and even assemblages of license plates.

But every approach carries a warning label, because no single method is foolproof. All I would suggest is that the further you deviate from what has traditionally been known to work, the bigger the hurdle you're creating for yourself.

If all approaches to writing fiction have one thing in common, it's this: the faith of the reader. And the reader, couched in innocence, will always assume we know exactly what we're doing, and that every detail we assign to a character is there for a reason. If we make a character thin or fat or tall or short, or partial to meatloaf or beer or the color yellow, the readers will assume we've included that detail as a signpost to keep them moving in the right direction. That's why arbitrary character details can foul things up: they send false messages. So when you go back to the gangly work of building and refining your own Freudian Potato Head, let the final draft be one in which you preserve every detail with a sense of purpose and intent, because in spite of what Freud himself might have claimed, in fiction a cigar is never just a cigar.

PLOT

Weave a Thick Rope, but Don't Hang Yourself

Even though plot can be a story's strong ally, it can also be an undermining foe. We probably all have a solid understanding of what plot is, at least in the most basic Aristotelean terms. Aristotle called it the "first principle," and his definition is the starting point for most conversations about plot. He described it as an arrangement of incidents into an "imitation of action." He also stipulated that this imitation of action should be something whole, something complete in itself. In other words, the actions should have a starting point, a natural line of development, and a finishing culmination—what we might call beginning, middle, and end. Furthermore, these parts should be bound together by a sense of dramatic unity, meaning that everything should be connected through causality. He observed that a sound plot would have so much structural unity that if a single element were removed, the story would become disjointed or disturbed.

His simple test for the efficiency of a plot was whether the events could be described as happening *after* one another or *because* of one another. A strong plot required uninterrupted causality. Such a plot could successfully hold a story together.

For many people, story and plot are synonymous terms. That's how we were first taught. As children we begged adults to read us stories, and for the most part those stories were comprised of little more than a tight plot of action, often with a moral in the end. *The Cat in the Hat* is a prime example of this story type, with each new advancement of the plot triggered by what we might snootily call structural causalities. But story is not quite the same thing as plot. In fact, depending upon whom you listen to, story is either something much simpler than plot, or something far more complex.

On the simple side, E. M. Forster defined story as simply "a narrative of events in their time-sequence," while plot was "also a narrative of events, the emphasis falling on causality." In other words, story could exist as a string of isolated events without any plot at all. My own view is that story is more comprehensive than that, and includes the totality of the storytelling elements—plot, character, setting, theme, and dialogue. Story covers not only the mechanics of what happens, but also the underlying causes and consequences.

It's important to note that Aristotle's analyses were never meant to be proscriptive, but merely descriptive. In other words, he wasn't trying to tell playwrights how to write plays, he was making observations about the successful plays that were being written. Like Galileo devising a telescope to view the planets, Aristotle was devising a lens through which we might observe principles already in place.

But Aristotle didn't have all the answers. In his world, plot was related solely to the external goings-on in a play—the events that moved the story forward. The story lines of Greek drama were created from linked actions that, for the audience, created a build-up of fear and pity for the central character. The plot would then reach its breaking point, the climax of the action, and deliver the audience, through resolution, into a state of catharsis. The simple fact is that we've come a long way since those early days of Greek theatre. Were Aristotle around today, he'd have a more complex storytelling landscape to contend with.

For the last seventy years or so, we've been in a state of story bombardment. Stories have come at us from so many sources we can hardly keep track. Besides books and theatre, we've had television, film, magazines, radio, role-playing board games, video games, social media. We've even listened to ghost stories around a campfire.

As a result, we've all become experts. Though you may not have thought consciously about it, you know story structure down to your bones. For you, the basic rom-com formula of *boy meets girl, boy loses girl, boy gets girl* might seem trite and out of date, but to the ancient Greeks that structure might have seemed a cutting-edge innovation. Readers as recent as the seventeenth century might have been exposed to a hundred plot-lines in the course of a lifetime, but you've borne witness to thousands upon thousands, so many that an "original" Aristotelean plot-line has become virtually nonexistent.

So how do we keep our work fresh, if all the plot options have grown stale? Well, first of all, we need to acknowledge that there are more types of plot lines available to us besides the plot of action that Aristotle championed. As literature has grown more subtle in its nuances of character and idea, we have developed the plot of character and the plot of thought.

The plays and short stories of Anton Chekhov paved the way for the plot of character, while philosophers like Albert Camus and Jean Paul Sartre moved us into plots of ideas. Both the plot of character and the plot of thought serve the same function as the plot of action in that all three involve maximal change. In other words, something has to be at stake for the character at the heart of the plot, and in playing itself out, the plot will alter the landscape it moves through.

In an action plot, James Bond has to save the world from an evil genius.

In a character plot, Holden Caulfield bumps through a series of episodes that reveal more and more about who he is and that ultimately bring about a change in the way he views himself and the world around him.

In a thought or idea plot, four characters in Raymond Carver's short story, "What We Talk about When We Talk About Love" sit around having drinks and discussing the nature of love until they're too drained to move, shaken to the core.

Granted, the plots of character and thought might be a little more challenging—even daunting—for the writer, because they're both rooted in the internal lives of the characters. It's easy to see where the tension comes from if Goldfinger or Dr. No is trying to blow up the world. It takes a more delicate and discerning hand to bring out the tension in a character having a personal crisis of faith, or battling depression, or contemplating the nature of the universe. The difficulty in writing these latter two forms of plot may explain why more people write action plots than the other two combined. But most of the enduring works of literature are in fact built on plots of character or plots of thought. William Faulkner, Virginia Woolf, Gertrude Stein, and James Joyce were all committed to plots of character and idea.

Of course, none of these plots are mutually exclusive. The same story can house two or three kinds of plot at once. Two writers who, for me, occasionally hit the trifecta of combining plots of action, character, and idea are Ernest Hemingway and Flannery O'Connor. I think that helps account for their longevity. But I've also seen plot multiplicity in the works of Anne Tyler, William Kennedy, Cormac McCarthy, Alice Walker, Toni Morrison, and many other contemporary writers. As audiences have become more sophisticated and discerning, writers have naturally become more complex in their approach to storytelling in general and plots in particular.

Let's not forget that plots do not have to be arranged chronologically. Though each action needs to come from character motivation, that motivation needn't be in response to the immediacy of the moment; motivation can just as easily come from a memory. Thus the chain of causality can come from something in the past, as well as something in the present. In other words, Bob might shed tears because he dropped an anvil on his foot, or Bob might shed tears because he sees an anvil, which reminds him of his long dead father, the blacksmith. Memories may direct a character's actions as clearly as present-moment circumstances. Much of contemporary fiction is structured as a back-and-forth exchange between the past and the present—which is to say, between the inner life and the external world—with each feeding off the other.

Remember that even in a character-based plot we have to keep our characters functioning in the world. Memories and thoughts lack power unless we have a context against which to measure them. Generally, the world around the character provides that context. A core of a story built on the inner monologue of a character wishing he could go outside for a walk will depend entirely on whether we're in the mind of a ninety-year-old on his deathbed or in the mind of a monkey in a cage. If a character muses on the beauty of a sunset, it makes a difference whether she's a blind woman, a prisoner awaiting execution, or a three-year-old child.

One definition of plot that can work for literary fiction is this simple: character interacting (internally or externally) with setting.

Because plots of all kinds are essentially consciously constructed patterns, plot may be called the product of intellect, rather than emotion. That means plot is an intellectual formulation of the relationships among incidents. It's a guiding principle for the author in moving forward, and a means of establishing order for the reader.

A guiding principle. That's especially important in a plot of thought or idea. When an abstract idea is the main concern of a story, there might be no coherent progression of action, no consistent cast list of characters. In such a plot we might, for example, get a series of vignettes involving different characters in different locales, with each vignette exploring an aspect of the same philosophical notion. Perhaps the plot is an examination of the nature of love, or god, or free will, or the universe, or the nature of reality. It might explore moral or ethical dilemmas. Beauty, truth, goodness. Evil, revenge, madness. Any cardinal virtue or mortal sin might be the subject of a plot of thought or idea. Such plots are not so much tied to the characters or events in a story, but to thematic issues. Perhaps an easy way to think of a plot of thought or idea is to approach it as a story in which theme dominates over action or character.

And of course we all know what theme is, because in high school that's how we were taught to approach literature. That's because there's a theme—or multiple themes—afoot in just about every piece of literature that survives from one generation to the next, whether it's *Moby Dick* or one of Aesop's fables. Theme is what lies at the heart of a story, the thing beyond the surface action that the story is about.

So what does theme have to do with plot? Well, plot is one means through which theme is conveyed. Think of plot as the train barreling along the tracks of your story. The theme is what the boxcars are loaded with, the content—what the story is about. At the same time, the rails supporting the train are made of theme, because theme is what keeps the plot on track. Any time your plot veers in an unexpected direction, ask yourself if the new direction reflects the theme of your story. If it doesn't, then you may be going off the rails.

In the Middle Ages there were dramatic productions called morality plays, which were dramatizations of basic moral principles. The characters weren't supposed to be idiosyncratic or original, they were supposed to be easily recognizable types. In fact, the central character of the most famous of these plays was named Everyman. In the course of the play, Everyman visits each of his friends to see who among them will accompany him on his journey into a realm called Death. His friends don't think Death sounds like much of a vacation spot. Sloth won't go with him. Neither will his friend Envy. Neither will Pride. Neither will any of his other friends whose names sum up their shortcomings. But just as Everyman is losing hope, a little friend he has long neglected volunteers to go with him. That friend's name is Good Deeds.

Notice that in this play there's no real depth or breadth of character. Each character represents a narrowly defined idea and becomes a mouthpiece for a point of view, a starting point for contemplation. There's still some causality in the story—the premise of Everyman's necessary journey triggers all the action that follows and provides a context for the line of thinking expressed by each character. The world around the character—the circumstance—becomes the wall against which the Ping-Pong ball of a single line of thought is constantly played. Such an approach to plot fulfills Aristotle's requirement of dramatic unity because everything is tied together thematically.

By contemporary standards, *Everyman* is a pretty lame theatrical effort. But there was a time when such a play was the talk of the mead hall. In the 1300s, audiences would have left the performance impressed, marveling that there had been a plot twist they never saw coming. We can't get away with such heavy-handedness today, except perhaps in Saturday morning cartoon shows. But we can still write a story based on the exploration of an idea, which is precisely what *Everyman* set out to accomplish.

Some great contemporary writers have taken this approach to plot. In *The Stranger*, Albert Camus was using his character as a sort of Everyman to explore a philosophical point of view. Some early stories of Hemingway's—like "Indian Camp" and "The End of Something"—do this, as well. Raymond Carver, Amy Hempel, and, well, thousands of other short story writers and novelists have explored the possibilities of the thought plot. One of my favorites is Alice Walker's story, "Everyday Use," which is an insightful (and moving) exploration of cultural priorities.

I suspect that the thought or idea plot is more common and effective in the short story form than in the novel, since the brevity of the short story may not require much of an action line at all. Some novels do succeed as vehicles of thought, but they're rare. Robert Pirsig's 1974 novel, *Zen and the Art of Motorcycle Maintenance: An Inquiry into Values,* stands as a towering example. So do the enlightenment novels of Carlos Castaneda—*The Teachings of Don Juan: A Yaqui Way of Knowledge*; *A Separate Reality*; and *Journey to Ixtlan.* On a less ponderous note, Richard Bach's two short novels, *Jonathan Livingston Seagull* and *Illusions* fit into this category, too. Each of these six novels became national best sellers, so don't think ideas have to make for dull reading.

Even the wacky stories and books of metafiction pioneer John Barth can qualify as thought plots, especially in the works in which he tries to explore the reaches of metafiction. Many of his short stories, in particular, can be viewed as essays about the craft of writing short stories. Other experimental writers have dabbled in the realm of the thought plot—Donald Barthelme, T. C. Boyle, Aimee Bender, Robert Coover,

Jorge Luis Borges, and Gabriel Garcia Márquez, to name but a few.

Granted, there's risk in allowing the thought plot to dominate your work. Some readers get frustrated when they can't locate the kind of plot they're used to, and they'll balk at reading nontraditional forms. If your own taste keeps you from trying your hand at such types of writing, there's nothing wrong with that. Just remember that the absence of an Aristotelean action plot in someone's work doesn't mean there's no plot there at all.

As I said earlier, these three types of plot—action, character, and thought/idea—are not mutually exclusive. You can have all three at once. There can be, and perhaps should be, plots developing on more than one level of your story. An action plot can keep the pace moving and introduce interesting twists to keep a reader moving forward. Simultaneously, a character plot might trace the way in which a character grows or evolves as a result of the external events of the action plot. Then, too, ideas can be developed along the way—psychologies, philosophies, and ideologies that build upon one another toward some larger, more complete understanding for the character or the reader.

My first writing teacher, the novelist Bynam Shaw, said the first step was "to have a cracking good story to tell." He's right, of course; all great literary art has to engage and entertain us or we won't keep reading. But the cracking good story—the Aristotelean action line—isn't enough. We also need to flesh out a character's line of growth and develop a thematic arc. In other words, to fulfill your implied contract with your readers, first get their attention (action plot), then give them something they can feel for (character plot), and then give them something worth thinking about (thought plot).

If you can cover those three bases, you'll have a solid piece of work. Each type of plot, if left to stand alone, may prove insufficient, because each has serious limitations. If all a story has going for it is an exciting action plot, the story can be fun, but it'll be no more nourishing than cotton candy. Interesting events can hold our interest, but in the long run they fail to satisfy any need beyond that of momentary distraction, like comic books from the 1950s.

If the entire focus of the story is on a character plot, giving us a deeply personal rumination from Grandpa while he sits in his rocker on the porch, we may get bored with the lack of external action, no matter how charming Grandpa himself might be.

The same risk of boredom holds true for the thought plot, which might easily become mired in abstract concepts. People don't read fiction because they're fans of philosophical essays. They want something to happen to somebody.

Okay, here's a brief lesson in American literary history about plot, and you'll probably hate that, but I feel obliged to include it, partly so you'll know when to nod knowingly during fancy dinner conversations, and partly so you'll understand how your own work fits into the picture, plot-wise. But feel free to cut class and skip the next fifteen paragraphs if you've had a hard day and just don't feel up to it.

Here we go:

In the early and mid-nineteenth century, the Romantics held firm to the Aristotelean model, structuring virtually every story as a chronological action plot. Poe, Hawthorne, Melville, and Robert Louis Stevenson all gave us good page-turners. They also threw in plenty of symbolism, most of it religious, but that was more the fashion of the day than an attempt at a thought plot. They believed in the God-governed universe, with an all-knowing, all-seeing, all-powerful Author pulling the strings on some of the all-time great action plots, many of which can be found in His best-selling book.

Then when literature evolved into Realism after the Civil War, plot fell into disrepute. The Realists were preoccupied with being true to life, and since life followed no discernible plot-line, plot as a literary convention became a minor annoyance to be largely overlooked.

The Realists, of course, hadn't really abandoned plot the way they imagined. They'd merely suppressed the Aristotelean approach, which allowed the plot of character to emerge. The focus shifted to the inner lives of rather dull, middle-class people as they lived lives in which not much happened beyond taking buggy rides in the country and sipping brandy in the drawing room.

By the way, plot wasn't the only thing the Realists left out. For all their talk of wanting to present life in a realistic fashion, they were a squeamish bunch who avoided any subject that might make a reader uncomfortable. The Civil War had left the entire country with a case of PTSD, and the purveyors of literature felt it might be best for the national psyche if they edited out all the messy or unpleasant things like violence, poverty, disease, and, of course, sex. Bottom line: Realism wasn't very realistic at all.

That avoidance of reality by the Realists was what gave rise to Naturalism, which by 1900 had set its course toward examining all the things the Realists had shied away from. The Naturalists wrote about war, prostitution, violence, and whatever ugliness they felt needed to be looked at, regardless of its unsavory nature. Whereas the Realists might show us someone being rude, the Naturalists would show us someone being brutal.

Along with all the boorish and ungentlemanly behavior, the Naturalists also brought along a return to the conventional action plot. They weren't Bible-thumpers, though, like the Romantics, they were primarily Freudians and Scientific Determinists who viewed fiction as a laboratory experiment, a controlled examination with a beginning, middle, and end. The idea was to study human nature, and the way to do that was to put a character under extreme stress and run him or her through a complicated plot-maze. The maze itself was more important than the character, because the maze—the environment—was ultimately responsible for shaping every aspect of behavior. Character was essentially reduced to the role of lab rat.

But then came World War I, and all bets were off. Along came the disillusioned, the disaffected, the embittered expatriots who bought into the world view articulated by Kierkegaard, Sartre, and Camus. These Existentialists provided the philosophical underpinnings for the next literary wave—Modernism, which was a doozy. The Modernists had little interest in the traditional conventions of literature, including the rules of grammar and syntax. They wanted to reinvent and revolutionize. Which they did.

For one thing, they resurrected the plot of character, especially in the stream-of-consciousness form, because they found the mind to be a more interesting and complex place to hang out than the outside world—especially if the mind in question was a little off-kilter.

But beyond that, they spotlighted and legitimized the plot of thought or idea—mainly because, well, they had a lot of thoughts and ideas, and plot innovations were part of that. Anyone asked to summarize the plot of Faulkner's *The Sound and the Fury,* or James Joyce's *Ulysses,* or just about anything written by Gertrude Stein would be hard pressed to come up with a simple answer. They showed us what it was like to plunge into the syntactical chaos of a disorganized mind. Sort of like Poe, but without the coherence.

If you've ever wondered what made Hemingway such a big deal in his day, it wasn't that he went to bullfights and shot a lot of big animals and got into drunken brawls even on weekdays. It was what he did on the page. He brought his journalist's to-the-point clarity to the Modernist sensibility. His protagonists were all existentialists—exemplars of the so-called *Hemingway*

Hero who rigidly adhered to a personal code of conduct, even in the face of certain death. That's what his thought plots were about—the existential need for each individual to construct and abide by a value system.

But like his fellow Modernists, he also was interested in developing the inner lives of his characters, so that their arc of interior change (the movement to what Joyce called the moment of *epiphany*) took center stage.

But wait, there's more—Hemingway was a big-time thinker, but he was also a big-time doer, and he understood the power of the old-fashioned plot of action.

So in Hemingway we get an engaging plot of action built upon interesting events, often involving life-and-death situations. Then that's combined with a plot of character involving exploration and growth, which gives us someone to care about, root for, and watch with fascination. And on top of all that, we get a backdrop of ideas being played out to a logical but unforeseen philosophical conclusion, which will give the reader something to wrestle with intellectually even after the story has reached its end.

If you can combine a plot of thought with a plot of character and wrap them both up in a plot of action, you'll have hit the trifecta. Readers appreciate a story that appeals on multiple levels.

But of course, nothing ever stays the same, even a theory that says everything needs to change. So Modernism gave way to something so confusing that we don't really know what to call it. All we can say for certain is that it's what came after Modernism, so we call it Postmodernism. In Postmodernism anything goes; all theories of art become equally valid, but also invalid. Want to nail a shoe to a billboard and call it a short story? Go ahead, nobody's stopping you. Let the reader make up a plot to go along with it.

So what does all this mean to you? It means you have a bigger bag of tricks to draw upon than you may have realized.

When Dennis Lehane made the move from writing traditional crime novels into his more literary works of *Mystic River* and *Shutter Island*, he didn't at all abandon the action plots that had served him well in earlier books. He simply added other levels. He built in a series of character plots for all his lead characters, showing their internal evolution. He set the books against a philosophical backdrop of the struggle between good and evil, or fantasy and reality—plots of thought that play out as powerfully as the plots of character and action.

My advice to you is to layer in more than one level of plot, because it will give your work more texture and depth. Let there be a rising action line for the external and internal worlds. For longer works, add in some subplots if you can—secondary lines of development that will give us reasons to care about secondary characters. Readers love complexity in storytelling, they love that moment when they recognize that, as we say, the plot thickens.

The advantages of weaving a thick rope of plot should be clear. But that thickness can also cause problems. Too much pre-plotting can strangle a story, especially in an action plot. If you decide beforehand everything that's going to happen, then the actual writing of the story can become as lifeless as filling out a tax form. You'll skim the surface and force characters to behave in ways dictated by the needs of the plot rather than by the natural psychologies of the characters. Forced action reduces characters to puppets. Once the reader stops believing in your character's motivations and subsequent actions, the story will die.

As a general rule, the more extreme the action, the longer the psychological runway you'll need in order to to make it fly. Any action can be made plausible, even actions that may at first appear to be out of character. Normally, the saintly nun won't attack a man on the street with a butcher knife. But if that's what the plot requires, you'll have to develop a thorough enough backstory and establish a clear enough context for us to view the attack as not only plausible, but natural. You might even need to make it seem inevitable.

It's also possible to pile on too many entanglements, so many that you can't find a plausible way out. There was a famous prime-time soap opera in the 1980s called *Dallas*, and during one season the writers piled on so many plot complications they couldn't write their way out of it. Their solution was to give themselves a do-over. Exercising the only cheesy option they had left, they had one of the characters wake up and find that the entire previous season had been a dream. None of the convoluted plot threads had to be continued. Problem solved. I suppose that, in a sense, that's nothing more than a natural step in the revision process—when you come to a dead end, throw out what isn't working and start again. But in their case, they had to let the entire country see their flawed first drafts. You won't have to suffer that embarrassment.

Some pre-plotting can be fine, though, especially at the level of establishing an overall basic structure. There's nothing wrong with having certain touchstones in mind as plot-points down the road. If you leave enough room between those plot points, you can find interesting and creative ways to get yourself believably from one point to the next.

Think of it like a cross-country trip in which you know you want to stop off in certain cities—say, Philadelphia, Columbus, New Orleans, Denver, and San Francisco. But instead of a roadmap, suppose you take only a compass. A trip like that will ultimately get you where you want to go, but the mile-by-mile and moment-by-moment uncertainty of the journey will keep it interesting, original, and unpredictable. Let yourself move forward on the plot line through exploration, rather than preconception.

And allow yourself to deviate at a moment's notice. Maybe something happens near Columbus that creates a worthwhile detour to Nashville. Maybe Nashville triggers a beeline to Memphis, and from there you decide to head on toward Denver, eliminating New Orleans from the trip altogether. Maybe the trip ends unexpectedly but appropriately in Denver, with no final push toward San Francisco at all.

Of course, some sub-genres might require a few more peeks at the roadmap than others. If you're writing a murder mystery, you have to write with the solution in mind. If you don't know who the killer is until the last page, then you haven't been planting the proper clues for the reader along the way. But even in such plot-bound narratives as the murder mystery, you can still leave yourself room to be creative with character, thought, and situation.

It could be that writer's block is merely the result of the writer's desire to know both the route and destination before actually making the trip. We want to write the last draft first, so we don't want to set down something we know we'll have to change later. But plot should be a complex thing, made up of many interwoven strands, and such complexity rarely comes out right in a first draft. A final plot must be arrived at through trial and error. It will need a sense of structure in the end, but knowledge of that structure doesn't have to be a precondition of starting the story. Structure can be discovered along the way.

That leap of faith is difficult for many inexperienced writers. I've encountered countless students who believe they can't start a story until they've figured out how to end it. I suspect if they were novice painters, they'd be more comfortable working from a paint-by-numbers kit than from a blank canvas. It takes courage to trust in the process of moment-by-moment discovery. But that's the pathway to art.

◆ ◆ ◆

Any discussion of plot would be incomplete without acknowledging Joseph Campbell's contribution to the conversation. Campbell was the comparative mythologist whose 1949 book, *The Hero with a Thousand Faces,* identified the prevailing storytelling structure—what one might call the uber-plot—that seems to be imbedded in our genes. He researched the enduring myths of as many cultures from around the world as he could find, both past and present. What he discovered was that the most important myths of every civilization have all followed basically the same plot and told the same story—a mono-myth that appeared worldwide, in culture after culture.

Whether you're talking about Buddha, Jesus, Moses, Harry Potter, Indiana Jones, Prometheus, Dorothy from *The Wizard of Oz,* Luke Skywalker, Neo from *The Matrix,* George Bailey from *It's a Wonderful Life,* or any romantic comedy ever made, you're talking about the same story.

The mono-myth unfolds in what playwrights or screenwriters would call a three-act structure. In the first act, the ordinary world is thrown out of balance and a reluctant hero receives the call to adventure. He then enters the special world—a point of no return—to begin the quest. Somewhere near the end of the first act or early in the second, the hero encounters a figure Campbell identifies as the "wise old man" who advises him—though in contemporary incarnations the figure doesn't have to be old, or even a man. A talking dog could fulfill the same function, as long as it said the right things at the right time.

The rest of act two is played out as a series of obstacles and crises involving allies and enemies, until finally the hero experiences the Dark Moment. The Dark Moment, which marks the end of act two, is the point at which the quest appears to have failed. But the third act sets things right. The hero rises up from apparent defeat, vanquishes the enemy, and restores the world to its previous sense of order.

Most of the fiction you've read and films you've watched conform to this basic plot structure, regardless of the genre. You've been exposed to this structure all your life. Think back to your nursery rhyme days. Even Mother Goose reflected the mono-myth.

> Hickory, dickory, dock,
> The mouse ran up the clock.
> The clock struck one
> The mouse ran down,
> Hickory dickory, dock.

That's perfect Campbellian structure. Hickory, dickory, dock is the ordinary world in balance. But the mouse runs up the clock entering the special world where he doesn't belong. The clock strikes one—the mouse's Dark Moment. He flees down the clock to safety, returning the world to balance again for the final hickory, dickory, dock.

Campbell, like Aristotle, was not telling us how we ought to structure our stories, or what plot framework we were supposed to employ, he was merely pointing out what he observed—that all cultures throughout recorded history have leaned heavily upon this storytelling form. The mono-myth seems to be something hardwired into our genes, and if that's indeed the case, even if you've never heard of Joseph Campbell, you probably have an innate appreciation for the story structure he described. Your stories might naturally conform to the mono-myth, simply because it resonates with us as a species. It's our default structure, the scaffolding supporting the most primal plot we've known. From cave-dwellers to Nobel Prize winners, the mono-myth has endured as a fan favorite.

Screenwriters tend to conform to Campbell's structure more consciously than fiction writers, mainly because screenwriting is part of a collaborative industry in which a great deal of money is often at stake. The novelist toils away on his or her own, and if a bad novel comes out of the process, it hasn't cost anything but the author's time. But in the film world, fortunes are routinely put at risk.

To protect their investments, production companies will keep a close eye on the writer every step of the way, and by contract they'll require the writer to conform to the three-act structure. Why? Because even if they've never heard of Joseph Campbell, they know to bank on stories that imitate previous successes. If audiences have historically responded well to a particular story structure, Hollywood will keep repeating that structure until it stops working. And the mono-myth never stops working.

George Lucas knew that well enough when he structured his epic 1977 space opera *Star Wars*. He even went so far as to have Joseph Campbell on set as an advisor.

But novelists tend to have more creative freedom than work-for-hire screenwriters, and most literary fiction writers would scoff at the notion of writing to fulfill a formula. They may, however, find Freytag's Triangle a slightly less objectionable way to describe dramatic action. In 1863 Gustav Freytag, through his study of Greek and Shakespearean drama, argued that effective dramatic structure consisted of five parts: exposition, rising action, climax, falling action, and resolution. He believed that plot needed to follow this template to be successful. I can't entirely disagree with the necessity of his five elements, though I think they can be juggled around a bit without damage to the story. But notice that nothing in Freytag's description, which sketches out as a triangle with the climax at the peak, is in violation of Campbell's mono-myth.

But, as I said, fiction writers needn't consciously conform to any of these descriptions of story structure. Carl Jung maintained that Campbell's plot points arose from archetypes that cut across all cultural boundaries. If he's right, then these identifiable structures may surface in your work whether you intend them to or not.

In either case, I don't think you should write with any external template in mind, especially in first drafts. That could end up as just another version of connect-the-dots, which might minimize exploration and discovery. Instead, I think you should simply try to write your most interesting stories. Then maybe you'll discover, after the fact, that your story naturally conforms to certain principles of effective storytelling. If, on the other hand, you find that your story isn't working, perhaps an awareness of Campbell's and Freytag's principles can be a useful starting point for your revisions.

Just don't let your initial plot twists and convolutions be set in stone. Revising plot lines is every bit as important as revising poor sentences and redefining character traits. Rework your plot until it serves your story's needs, letting each moment lead naturally to whatever would logically follow from it. Instead of letting plot dominate, let it be an equal partner among the other elements of fiction in the creation of an organic whole. Plot can be a tool to reinforce character, setting, language, and theme to sustain the dramatic unity. If you achieve that, you'll have created a work of art.

5

SETTING

The Hydrogen Atom of Fiction

If you'll remember back to 7th or 8th grade, whenever it was that they started putting that chart of the periodic table up on the wall in your early science classes, you may recall that the most basic element was the hydrogen atom. It was the simplest atom on the chart, the most elemental of elements, the atom reduced to its most basic form.

As you certainly know by now, we have elements in fiction. Not as many as the periodic table, but each of them is an essential component of the fiction universe. You can write a story without certain elements, but if you do, you'll be increasing your chances of failure.

Some writers put character as the most important element, while others may give top billing to plot. Theme is an important element because it adds depth, giving fiction more than a superficial meaning. Dialogue is one of the basics. Elsewhere on our chart we may find exposition, description, and pace. Point of view. Tone and mood. Maybe style itself appears somewhere, though style is more a complex molecule than one of the atoms.

But nothing that I've listed so far qualifies as the hydrogen atom of fiction, the most basic building block of all. For that, we have to look to what may be the most undervalued of elements, the one we tend to view more as a chore than as an opportunity: setting.

Think of the most archetypal Old Testament stories. If Adam and Eve aren't in the Garden of Eden, they're just another bickering couple. Setting establishes their stakes and lends significance to the actions of both characters.

Who is Noah without a flood? Just a deranged ship builder. Setting elevates his actions and casts him in the role of a great preserver of life.

Who is Lot without the destruction of Sodom and Gomorrah? Just a better-than-average man in a worse-than average town.

When Moses announced the seven plagues that devastated Egypt, his warnings were all about setting and the damage it could do. Later, when he parted the Red Sea, that use of setting demonstrated that he was more than just the leader of a gang of runaway slaves.

Jesus is often presented through the shorthand of his most important settings: his Baptism in the River Jordan, the Sermon on the Mount, the Garden of Gethsemane, the Last Supper, the Cross.

In a more literary vein, Milton focused on *Paradise Lost,* Dante on *The Inferno.* Cervantes wrote about Don Quixote jousting with windmills. A quick scan of the table of contents of any major short story anthology will yield a great number of titles that refer specifically to setting. Among them you are likely to find "Hills Like White Elephants," "The Open Boat," "A Worn Path," "The Ones Who Walk Away from Omelas," "Why I Live at the P.O.," "Where I'm Calling From," "Shiloh," "The Yellow Wallpaper," "In the Cemetery Where Al Jolson Is Buried," "Cathedral," "The Fall of the House of Usher," "Murders in the Rue Morgue," "Araby," "Occurrence at Owl Creek Bridge," "A&P," and "How I Contemplated the World from the Detroit House of Correction and Began My Life Over Again."

In the examples I've just cited, setting is never just a static backdrop against which a story plays out. Rather, it's an active participant in the story, a dynamic element. In all of these examples, character interacting with setting is what generates the plot.

Setting is at the heart of so much of what we do, and yet we take it for granted. Often when we set about to write a story or a novel we approach setting as a necessary chore, the furniture we have to put in the room so the characters will have a place to sit down. We toss in lifeless descriptions of what things look like, because, as we know from every writing class we've ever taken, it's better to *show* than to *tell*. But there's no excitement in that kind of descriptive work, no dramatic tension. Setting should not be something left in the background, it should be something a character has to contend with.

Years ago at the Vermont College of Fine Arts I was just beginning a lecture on setting when someone on the college's grounds crew cranked up a chainsaw just outside the window. He had hedges that needed some severe pruning, and because of some swelling in the sashes from humidity, the window wouldn't close. For twenty minutes I had to fight against the racket of the chainsaw to try to get my message across.

What I finally realized was that the setting of my lecture itself had provided me with the best object lesson I could have hoped for. The environment of the lecture was intruding upon the lecture, and that's exactly what setting should do in your fiction. There should be some version of that chainsaw outside the window of every story you write.

Yet most inexperienced writers fail to realize that setting is not a chore at all, but an opportunity. To begin with, setting probably covers a lot more ground than you think. Sure, it's the furniture in the room, and that may seem like a boring place to start. But remember that the objects that surround a character can speak volumes about who the character is. A character whose apartment walls are painted white is not the same as a character whose apartment walls are painted black or striped or polka-dotted or covered in murals depicting the death of Pancho Villa. So there's a couch in the room—but is it a yard-sale acquisition or an expensive couch inherited from a beloved grandparent? Does the art work on the walls come from Picasso, Van Gogh, or Disney? Or are there just photos of family vacations? Is there a velvet Elvis in the living room? Or pictures of cacti? Is the yard well-trimmed or has it been taken over by weeds? That car in the driveway—is it a rusted clunker or a sleek new Italian sports car? Every physical object and condition in your character's life tells us something about who the character is—which is why they should never be thrown in arbitrarily.

But that's only on the most basic level of setting. Besides the physical surroundings, we have conditions of time and place to consider. It makes a difference whether your story is set today or in the 1940s. It makes a difference whether your story takes place in the dead of winter in Maine or the middle of summer in Key West.

Imagine a man sitting in a diner waiting to be joined by his fiancée, who is late. If there's a driving rainstorm outside and bridges in the area have been washed out, that adds tension to the scene. In this instance, setting disrupts the calm of the characters' world. It intrudes.

Setting should also include the sociological and cultural elements that put pressure on a character. A childhood in the Bible Belt is different from one spent in the Rust Belt or Silicon Valley. It matters whether the character grew up rich or poor. If a character is religious, the brand of religion matters, because there are serious differences between Catholicism, Judaism, Islam, Hinduism, and whatever label goes with an evangelical backwoods snake-handler. The son of a plumber might be brought up in a different environment than the son of a four-star general or a pot farmer. A character raised in a single-parent household might have a very different life from one brought up in an orphanage.

It's not difficult to see that much of what we would call a character's backstory is an extension of setting. Setting can legitimately include everything that contributes to the atmosphere and environment in which the character is formed. That's what makes setting such an opportunity. It's a chance for you to bring in the whole world to shape your character's identity and move your plot along.

Setting can even be a mainstay of theme. In a story like Hemingway's "Hills Like White Elephants," for example, the setting presented to us in the title tells us more about the story than anything in the story itself. Those hills are what T.S. Eliot would have called an *objective correlative*. That is, they're the symbolic representation that contains the core of what the story is about. In the story, a couple discusses what to do about an unwanted pregnancy. The hills suggest the roundness of the pregnant belly. The fact that the hills are white rather than green suggests the opposite of fertility, a linking of fecundity and barrenness—a doomed pregnancy. And the idiomatic term "white elephant" refers to some unwanted gift one is forced to deal with. Thus the entire story is laid out for us by the setting against which the story unfolds.

We should also keep this in mind about setting: it carries much of the visual element of a story. The visual dimension is crucial for many reasons, but chief among them is memorability. Yes, we all want to develop lofty intellectual concepts in our fiction so we might be mistaken for geniuses, but the simple fact is that abstractions evaporate quickly from a reader's mind. If you want your ideas to last, you need to house them in something concrete, something the mind can picture, because if the mind can see it, the mind can hold on to it.

The staying power of the visual—that's why the ancient Chinese book of philosophy, the *I Ching*, was constructed from sixty-four images, most of which were representations of setting. Pictures borrowed from nature cannot be undone by the evolution of language across time and cultures. Fire on the mountain, water over the earth, wood over water—these are enduring images, the clarity of which won't erode from one generation to the next.

Similarly, it's no accident that throughout history the great teachers have conveyed their ideas through visually based stories, because actions in the context of a setting can survive even a weak translation. Plato developed the Allegory of the Cave. Jesus taught in parables. Confucius relied heavily on the images of the *I Ching*. They each understood that concreteness is the strongest housing for a principle or idea. Abstraction is weak, even when it's right. One might say that war is ugly, and we might agree with that abstract statement. But give us a description of a soldier's intestines strung out across a bloody stretch of battlefield, and the notion of war being ugly takes on a heightened level of power.

Don't undervalue what setting can do for your fiction. Use it as a dynamic element, not a passive one. Let setting apply pressure to character; let it force turns of plot; let it symbolically reflect your themes. Think of it, if you will, as an extra conscious presence in the story, one which exerts its will in every direction, upon every player on the stage. Let setting be a secret force, an omnipresent means through which the writer may wield a controlling hand.

But even though I rank setting as the most elemental of the elements of fiction, that doesn't mean you should lead with it in your stories. Necessary though they may be, descriptions of trees, architecture, and weather aren't the most engaging of your story's building blocks. First, hook us on a character and a situation, then color in the world around them.

6

DIALOGUE

Enough said

On the surface, dialogue would seem to be the easiest element of craft to handle successfully. We all know how to talk. Without any rehearsal, we can volley back and forth for hours, carrying on seamless conversations into the wee hours of the morning. We can do it sick, drunk, or half asleep. It's easy. Not surprising, then, that it's also ridiculously simple to fill page after page with believable dialogue.

And that's what makes writing dialogue so difficult.

"Hi, Bob. How's the weather up there in Walla Walla?"

"Oh, just fine, Bill. Marjorie works in her garden a lot, and I do a lot of yard-work myself. What's new with you and Eileen?"

"Well, we both love the new season of television shows, and I'm thinking of buying a new pair of running shoes because my old ones have a hole on one side. It's not a big hole. About the size of a pea. On the left shoe. The right one is okay. I may get a different kind of shoelace this time, though. I'm tired of those flat laces, so I think I'll try the round kind, if I can find them in a good color. Maybe an off-white, something like eggshell. Or maybe I'll go all the way to beige."

Ad nauseam, ad infinitum. It's the very ease with

which we can put words into characters' mouths that makes good dialogue deceptively hard to create—and dangerous to the survival of your story. The above conversation between Bob and Bill does nothing but take up space. And that's not acceptable.

Keep in mind that dialogue is not conversation. Real world conversation is almost always packed with filler. Not just the *ums* and *wells,* 99.9% of which should be taken out, but also the unnecessary bits of information, redundancies, and digressions. In a satirical critique of his own early work, the poet Albert Goldbarth observed that he "never used one word when ten would do." We all share in that tendency at one time or another. We're comfortable with dialogue, and so we rely on it more than we should.

I think of it as a Jamesean problem. In Henry James' day, as I've noted, the Realists promoted art as a mimetic exercise, copying life as closely as possible. If one seeks to imitate real life in fiction, then the inclusion of rambling, pointless conversations would seem a natural part of the process. But we've come a long way since James and his Realists. Today's audiences are more savvy, more experienced, and more impatient.

Bad dialogue is not a recent problem, however. Even Shakespeare wrote some bad dialogue—dialogue that sacrificed character for exposition, or dialogue that strained against natural speech so much as to become comically obtuse.

Take for example this bad exchange in the play *Hamlet* between Laertes and Gertrude. It's late in the play, and Laertes is furious over the death of his father, Polonius. Laertes's only surviving relative is his beloved sister, Ophelia, whom he loves more than his own life. But Gertrude comes to Laertes and delivers the sad news: "Your sister's drowned, Laertes," she tells him. And what is Laertes's response? "O, where?" he asks. By any measure that's a dopey and unrealistic reaction. Shakespeare had a reason, of course. He was using

Laertes as the straight man to set up a poetic description of the death scene by Gertrude, a more important character. Gertrude answers Laertes's stupid question with a beautiful set piece, the famous, "There is a willow grows aslant a brook" speech. Then, when Gertrude has finished her lengthy, point-by-point account of Ophelia's drowning, Laertes compounds his idiocy with another unlikely line: "Alas, then she is drowned?" Yes, you moron, that fact was just established at great length. Sorry to buck so many centuries of Shakespeare idolatry, but there's no getting around the fact that in this case the Bard sacrificed the emotional plausibility of one character so another one could give us a pretty monologue. Don't do that in your work. Learn from Shakespeare's blunders.

It's a common flaw, one which virtually every writer has fallen victim to at one time or another. We force our characters to say what the plot requires, or we force them to become expository mouthpieces. In so doing, we forget what should be our most important concern for any character—that he or she be a *person* speaking the lines, not just a *puppet* of the author in service of plot or exposition.

Such lapses were rare on Shakespeare's part. Hamlet's sidekick Horatio serves a functional role as Hamlet's confidant, asking the right questions and giving the necessary warnings. But Horatio is also a fleshed-out character with noble qualities of his own. He isn't merely a functionary, he's a *person* who happens to fulfill some functions along the way. Osric, the fop in the play, is a functionary who rises above that limitation with a memorable personality. Polonius is a functionary who serves as the sounding board for both Claudius and Gertrude, but he's also a rounded character with his own comically idiosyncratic traits.

The secret to having functionaries become people—whether in drama or fiction—lies in giving them enough of a subtext, enough of a backstory, to provide a personal motivation for whatever the character says or does. The words that come from a character's mouth need to be a natural extension of that character, not just an expression of the author's needs for the text.

Good dialogue is a distillation of language appropriate to character and situation. Remove the chit-chat. Clear away the debris and let dialogue do its jobs. Those jobs fall into at least five distinct functions.

Reveal exposition or backstory:
"Marvin, I haven't seen you since high school."

Reveal character and relationships:
"Marvin, I thought you were my best friend until you turned me in for cheating on that algebra test."

Reveal or advance the plot:
"Marvin, let's take a ride out to the quarry. There's some business there I need to take care of."

Reveal emotion or attitude:
"Marvin, I'm glad you came with me to the quarry. Very glad indeed."

Reveal theme:
"Marvin, I meant to throw you into the quarry. But revenge can't change the past. I see that now. You weren't the one who kept me out of Harvard, I was.

Obviously, these examples are a little clunky. And even though they do each illustrate a single function of dialogue, that makes them too elementary to pass for good dialogue. Good dialogue should always address more than one of these jobs at a time.

Notice that each of these five jobs included the word *reveal*. That's the common mission of all dialogue. The point of dialogue is to reveal things. It must pull back the covering and show the heart, the core, whatever lies below the surface. That's why chit-chat is almost always ineffective—it's stuck at the superficial level.

Ah, you say, *but what if my characters are supposed to be superficial?* Well, if your characters are supposed to be superficial, how can we learn to respect them, root for them, care about them? Superficiality is fine for a minor character, a functionary, characters we aren't supposed to connect with in any meaningful way. But major characters should usually not be left at a superficial level of development.

And the same goes for chatty drunks and stoners. While it's true that in real life drunks and stoners might blab endlessly about silly, irrelevant things, in art that's empty dialogue. Unless the state of intoxication causes the drunk to reveal something important, we'll probably find listening to aimless babble annoying.

That's also true for glib, witty characters. I've occasionally run across students who try to make all their characters sound like the lead in a Noel Coward play, overly sophisticated and cleverly sharp-tongued, bantering back and forth as if the story were a verbal fencing match. But clever repartee is not necessarily good dialogue. It can be, of course, in certain circumstances. But for the most part, a stream of witticisms can obscure who a character really is. The clown mask can prevent us from connecting with the person behind it. The occasional clever line can be great. An endless stream of them can reduce the character to a nightclub act.

Give all your creations distinct voices. The more a voice emerges as distinct and even idiosyncratic, the stronger the character behind it will become—as long as you don't resort to phony or exaggerated dialects. William Carlos Williams gives us a fine example of voice in his poem, "The Last Words of My English Grandmother." A title like that sets us up for some sentimental Hallmark Card moment, and we enter the poem expecting something emotional and wise. But at the end of the poem, as the cantankerous and rather disagreeable grandmother is being loaded into an ambulance, Williams gives us her final words: "What are those fuzzy looking things out there? Trees? Well, I'm tired of them." That's great dialogue because it's unexpected—yet still true to the cantankerous, complaining person the grandmother has been throughout the narrative.

Remember, readers want characters to say something they haven't heard before. They want *real,* but they also want *original.* Trite phrases abound in life, but they shouldn't in fiction. The fact that real people talk in mundane ways is no excuse to let your characters tread water in a familiar pool of language. It isn't enough for dialogue to be realistic; it must be fresh, and it must be meaningful.

Though this may sound like an odd approach to writing dialogue, here's a rule I impose upon myself: I never use dialogue unless I have to. I came to this position, strangely enough, through screenwriting. Contrary to popular impression, screenplays aren't built upon exchanges of dialogue. Dialogue is only there to accomplish what the action cannot. That's because screenplays have always been primarily a visual, rather than a spoken medium. Dialogue is the mortar between the bricks of a film, not the bricks themselves.

A truism of the screenwriting genre is that if dialogue doesn't advance the story, it should be cut—no matter how witty, clever, or entertaining it may be. The story—and I believe this applies to fiction, as well—should be forced along at a good pace by pared-down dialogue, not slowed to a crawl by long-winded speeches. Audiences lose interest in characters who converse in paragraphs. So unless your story is based on the Lincoln-Douglas debates, keep dialogue exchanges brief. A pithy observation can have a more powerful effect than a treatise.

An exception can always be made for a minor or supporting player. It's fine to define a secondary character by his foolish babbling, or his dry, pedantic orations, but that can be difficult to pull off in a major character. It's not impossible, but it's rare.

Resist the impulse to over-explain. Suggesting something can be more intriguing than flatly stating it. As William Blake observed, *That which can be made explicit to the idiot is not worth my care.* Assume your reader is every bit as smart as you are.

And here's a radical thought: sometimes it's best for a character just to keep his mouth shut. The most common line that appears in all of Hemingway's short stories is this three-word declaration: *Nick said nothing.*

I'd recommend letting that be your first thought with every character who is on the verge of speaking. *Marvin said nothing. Emily said nothing.* Then, if it's clear that the character has to say *something*, go for the minimal, the least that can be said beyond nothing. As a frame of mind, that will force you to keep your dialogue lean and meaningful, because when your character finally says something, it really will be *something.*

A common mistake I see in student work is to waste dialogue on things we already know. Dialogue should open up new territory, not restate the obvious. For example, if a character who is trying to steal a car from a car lot gets caught by a security guard, it would be bad dialogue to have the security guard say, "Ha! You were trying to steal a car, but I caught you!" We already know that. But if instead the security guard says, "You think your Aunt Della can handle this, on top of everything else?" that opens up the story in fresh ways. It tells us things about the relationship between the guard and the robber, and raises questions about the world beyond the crime itself. Good dialogue will keep a reader looking ahead.

Even when a necessary conversation takes place in the story, the reader might not need to hear every word of it. Sometimes it's better to reduce dialogue to summary, delivering the substance of the conversation indirectly. If one character has to fill another one in on things we already know, for example, don't take us through the process, just give us the gist: *Jim told Harriet about the fiasco at the airport.* This is also a useful tactic for avoiding mundane aspects of a dialogue exchange: *Bob rambled on for a while, waiting for the right moment to tell Heather what had happened to her chihuahua.*

Too often I've seen writers make the mistake of substituting dialogue for the more difficult work of supplying setting and action. That's an abuse. Don't let dialogue be your escape clause from writing fully fleshed out sequences of moment-by-moment action. Rarely can a story hold our attention if characters are doing nothing but sitting around discussing things. There are some wonderful exceptions, of course, but as a rule readers want to see characters doing something, interacting physically with the world. A man talking about the pointlessness of his life while sitting in an easy chair in his living room is less engaging than a man talking about the pointlessness of his life while cleaning the third-story gutters on his roof, or driving a friend to the hospital, or chasing a pack of coyotes from his back yard. Just because there's dialogue doesn't mean the rest of the world stops spinning.

And keep in mind that sometimes simply smashing a vase can say more than a two-page speech.

Dialogue should be natural, but it should also be essential—and I mean that in the purest dictionary sense. Essential: so important as to be indispensable; fundamental; vital; cardinal; something upon which an outcome turns or depends.

Dialogue wasn't always natural. All literary genres trace their roots to poetry, and poetry existed prior to what we now call *paper*. Thus, the oral tradition was the starting point for all forms of storytelling. Meter and rhyme provided an easy framework for remembering a text word for word so stories could be passed down from one generation to the next. That made for some memorable but awkward dialogue. People don't naturally speak in verse.

But technology changed all that. The invention of paper and the printing press, and later the nearly universal ability to read and write allowed dialogue to leave its roots of sing-song rhyme and evolve into more natural forms of expression.

Ideally, the voice of the character is usually separate from the voice of the writer. But what exactly is voice, anyway? Well, it's a combination of tone, attitude, world view, diction, and style that conveys personality. Voice is the opposite of classic reportage, which seeks to become generic and anonymous. In a good modern newspaper, each news article should sound like it came from the same reporter, even though there may be twenty reporters contributing to every issue. The "invisible" reporter was a standard convention for most of the nineteenth and twentieth centuries, during which time only columnists and editors developed identifiable voices. That changed in the 1960s when New Journalists like Joan Didion allowed the personal voice to creep in, and Gonzo Journalist Hunter S. Thompson allowed it to take over altogether. A century before Didion or Thompson, Mark Twain had an early editorial voice as distinctive as that of any of the characters he would later go on to create. But whether we're talking about writer or character, voice still comes down to one thing: it's what provides our sense of the person behind the words.

Unless you're writing dialogue for a buffoon, don't artificially inflate your language. Clarity is more important than flowery phrasing. Power comes from using the exact word, not some distant cousin you found in a thesaurus. Don't tell someone to *eschew obfuscations* if all you mean is *be clear.*

To return to poor Laertes again, there's an example

of this type of error in Act 4, Scene 7 of *Hamlet.* Laertes, in plotting with the King against Hamlet, utters this tortured sentence:

> I bought an unction of a mountebank,
> So mortal that, but dip a knife in it,
> Where it draws blood no cataplasm so rare,
> Collected from all simples that have virtue
> Under the moon, can save a thing from death
> That is but scratched withal: I'll touch my point
> With this contagion, that if I gall him slightly,
> It may be death.

In other words, "I bought some poison I can put on my sword; that'll kill him for sure." Granted, my version may not have Shakespeare's elegance, but at least it wouldn't leave the groundlings scratching their heads. And the King's response is hardly more clear:

> Weigh what convenience both of time and means
> May fit us to our shape: if this should fail,
> And that our drift look through our bad
> performance,
> 'Twere better not assay'd: therefore this project
> Should have a back or second, that might hold,
> If this should blast in proof.

Huh? Okay, I get the gist, but still. Clearly, Shakespeare had some off days.

Hamlet did have some good advice to offer us about dialogue, though. In Act 3, Scene 2, he advises the players to:

> Speak the speech, I pray you, as I pronounced it to you, trippingly on the tongue. But if you mouth it, as many of your players do, I had as lief the town crier spoke my lines.

That's good advice for all of us. Don't let your characters soullessly mouth words. No character should be reduced to the role of town crier—a stilted mouthpiece for exposition. Let each character be a person of flesh and blood who speaks naturally, and from the heart.

But succinctly. Any time you write a line of dialogue, examine it with this question in mind: *Does this really need to be said?* Often, our dialogue is an explicit statement of things that we've already made implicit. Trust your reader to get the implied elements of the story without any rehashing of the ideas through dialogue.

If you believe the line needs to be said, then ask yourself this: *Does it reveal something new?* Dialogue that reveals nothing might need to be rethought.

If you're sure that a line is indeed necessary and revelatory, ask yourself the next question: *Is there a shorter way to say it?* Wordiness is rarely a virtue, except as a comic character trait. Sometimes a brief sentence fragment is the more effective form of expression.

Then once you're satisfied that you've written the line with the brevity it deserves, ask yourself this: *Does it require a response from another character?* A single line left hanging in the air can be far more effective than the page of predictable dialogue that might naturally follow from it.

In short, let your potential speakers struggle to keep their secrets. Very few memorable main characters in literature have been blabbermouths.

ENDINGS

Are We There Yet?

As we've noted, the enduring stories are quest narratives, and a quest is a journey. In many of our most revered stories, the journey is easy to spot. *The Iliad* and *The Odyssey,* for starters: everybody goes off to war, then everybody tries to get home. Then there's Don Quixote, who travels the countryside looking for his beloved Dulcinea. Or *The Divine Comedy,* in which Dante takes us on a tour of the organizational structure of the underworld. In Tolkien's *The Lord of the Rings,* a small band of misfits must traverse the most lethal landscape ever written. In Jules Verne's *Around the World in Eighty Days,* some adventurers set out to go around the world in. . . well, you know. Closer to our own time, Huckleberry Finn takes a trek with Jim down the Mississippi. Then there's *On the Road* by Jack Kerouac. Or, more recently, just *The Road,* by Cormac McCarthy.

But these examples are obvious choices, because the narratives are built around characters who need to get from point A to point B—or if not point B exactly, then at least somewhere other than point A. When they arrive at that second point, the story winds down to its anticipated close. When Odysseus gets home from his travels, we know all he has left to do is pet his dog, kill his wife's suitors, and settle into a peaceful retirement. Frodo doesn't even have to do that much when he gets back from dropping off the Ring of Power in Mount Doom.

But what about stories that aren't carrying the burden of being cultural milestones—those earnest pieces of fiction we're all struggling to write? Our characters may not be out there tilting at windmills, at least not literally, but they're on the move, nevertheless. I believe all good stories are journeys, even if none of the characters ever gets up out of a chair.

In Raymond Carver's short story, "What We Talk about When We Talk About Love," nobody ever goes anywhere, physically, but all four characters are left exhausted at the story's end. That's because, without ever leaving the room, they've covered a lot of difficult emotional territory. The same holds true in Carver's "Cathedral," in which a quiet living room conversation between a blind man and a low-class lout transports the lout to a heightened level of empathetic awareness. That's what every good story does: it covers emotional or psychological ground. The more difficult the ground, the better.

So there we are, breezing along the highway of our tale. Sometimes we're chugging slowly uphill, sometimes we're coasting down the easy slopes, and sometimes we're barreling across the flatlands. But where's our exit ramp? How do we know when we've gotten to wherever it is we're going?

The answer differs according to genre. If you're writing a murder mystery, you have to know your exit beforehand, and the story pretty much has to end after the killer has been identified and apprehended. We have no interest in hanging around with the brilliant sleuth after the sleuthing is over. Once the mystery has been solved, I don't need to watch Sherlock Holmes and Dr. Watson play a celebratory game of badminton at the

Club. After the villain has been led away in handcuffs, I don't need to accompany Miss Marple to her podiatrist to watch her have her corns removed. When you write mystery stories, your route is mapped out ahead of time, your ending is predetermined, and all you have to do is follow your own road signs.

But literary fiction is a different trip entirely. You're driving at night, for one thing, and your headlights extend only a few feet into the darkness. There might not be any street signs, which makes it easy to take a wrong turn and get lost. The exit you're looking for could easily be missed.

But here's something to reassure you: no matter where you are in a story, the end is always in sight.

Wait. I've said, "*the* end is always in sight," when I should have said, "*an* end is always in sight." Because for any given literary story, there may be an infinite number of ways to end it, depending on how long you wish the story to be, and how resolutely you've kept to the roadway.

Now, what do I mean by keeping to the roadway? I'm talking about staying true to your themes, to what the story is about. That's because you can't properly end a story unless there's thematic consistency to support it. Having a meteor come crashing down out of the blue to kill off your main character might *stop* your story, but it won't *end* it. And if all you've done is wander aimlessly through a wide-open story desert where no theme is established so you can't tell a path from a digression, it's impossible to arrive anywhere. That kind of material is what we call *pre-writing,* and none of it may belong in the final version of the story; it's just your search for the right beginning. Without the right beginning, you can't establish any kind of forward path, and if there's no identifiable forward path, there can be no culmination of experience, which means you're no closer to an ending on page thirty than you were on page three. Where there is no sense of direction, there is no destination. So the first step in arriving at an ending is to make sure you've written a coherent story that deserves one, a story that has dramatic and thematic unity. Proper endings have to be earned.

That requires some discipline on the writer's part. Say you're writing a story about misdirected love. Any number of angles might be explored: the loss of self-identity, the potential pain of betrayal, the distraction from career, maybe even the destruction of a family. All kinds of things might belong in such a story, and you might write all kinds of scenes exploring the different facets of the theme. But maybe that scene about doing crossword puzzles, and the one about learning to water ski, and the one about painting the house might not belong—unless, of course, you can find a way to make those scenes relevant to the story's core. If you can't, then they're digressions and they don't belong, no matter how funny or moving or exciting they may be.

That doesn't mean you should throw those irrelevant scenes away. Sooner or later you'll write a story in which they *can* be made relevant, so save them for a time when they'll matter. After all, there must be something of value in them, or else you wouldn't have had the impulse to write them in the first place.

Each scene should be linked with all the others through thematic unity, with each one adding some new perspective on whatever the theme may be. Otherwise, you're just moving aimlessly (if the scenes are thematically disconnected), or else redundantly (if the scenes are revisiting facets you've already addressed).

There's an important distinction to make here, and that's the difference between randomness and spontaneity. The two are often confused. You probably realize that predictability is a bad thing. You don't want your readers guessing the end of your story before you get there—which is one thing literary fiction has in common with the murder mystery. Good literary fiction, however, should have far more options for potential endings than a murder mystery, since there will always be a small and finite number of suspects for Miss Marple or Sherlock Holmes to consider. In literary fiction the possible outcomes are as limitless as life, so there's no excuse for predictability. If your reader can outguess you, then you've been too heavy-handed in putting up signposts along the way, or else you've set up the story as a limited duality (*Will she take the job or won't she? Will they get married or won't they? Will the ship sink or won't it?*)

But some inexperienced writers, in order to avoid predictability, assume that random action is the cure. There's logic to that, I suppose. If you push ahead chaotically, there's no way for the story to become predictable. But that also means there's probably no ending that can unite all those random steps into a unified whole, bringing coherence to the journey. As Aristotle would insist, there must ultimately be a dramatic unity of action, time, and place.

So what's the answer? Move forward without knowing where you're going, but with a firm knowledge of what the story is about. Let every paragraph be a new discovery, let your direction unfold organically as you explore your chosen topic. Call it controlled spontaneity.

Sounds contradictory, I know. But think of it this way. Suppose you're traveling with a car full of kids for an eight-hour drive. They might do any number of things on the journey—sing songs, pose riddles to one another, tell jokes, finish their homework, listen to music, play video games, or even stage a backseat version of *Macbeth*. There's literally no telling what things they might do, or what order they might do them in. But you'll always keep them inside the car. That's the part you can plan for ahead of time, the part you can control. As long as you keep them in the car, they'll be covering ground toward the destination.

Your story, then, is a carload of unruly children. Let them play whatever games they want to play, but keep them in the car at all times. Let your characters behave in whatever spontaneous ways you might discover for them to behave, but confine their behavior to what the story is about. Sure, from time to time you might stop to let a kid use the restroom; just don't let him catch a ride in another car, because that would be a digression on the journey—a different story altogether.

Now, let's assume you've done that. You've eliminated the digressions and kept your story focused on moving forward along the path of spontaneous discovery. Your story is deserving of an ending. So how do you know what it is?

Well, before we can answer that, we need to raise a question about the length of the journey. The fact is, sometimes we know the approximate length of our journey and sometimes we don't. There are times when we know we're working on a novel, and if that's the case, we probably won't start looking for an ending on page seven, or even page 107. At times we know we're writing a short story, which may leave us more open to an early discovery of an exit route. Sometimes we can assign ourselves exercises of specific lengths to develop a feel for story arcs. I've even assigned one-page stories. I do that for many reasons, but mainly it's to force the writer to decide what has to be present in order for a thing to be called a complete story. One page isn't a lot to work with, so "story" tends to get boiled down to its essence.

How short can a story be? There's a poignant six-word story that has often been attributed to Hemingway, though his connection to the piece is questionable:

> For sale: baby shoes, never worn.

Here, the first line is also the last line; the end is contained in the beginning. Though Hemingway himself may not have penned the words, the story epitomizes what Hemingway stood for—a clear focus with no wasted language, no deviation from what the story is about. After these six words, nothing more need be said, and any further elaboration would merely weaken the ending. The author arrived at the perfect moment of departure.

Sometimes that happens to us all. We look down at our story with wide-eyed surprise, discovering that we've reached the perfect ending without knowing it was coming. Such happy accidents should be treasured. But we shouldn't count on such effortless conclusions any more than we should count on the accurate strike of a meteor.

In a one-page story, if we start with that limitation as our goal, we can pretty much control the story from the outset. Usually, such a piece will focus on a single moment of clarity in a character's life, with just enough backstory thrown in to establish a context to make the clarity meaningful. That's easy to accomplish in a single page.

But no one makes a habit, much less a career, out of writing one-page stories. In longer pieces, the precise end-point is a little more difficult to predict. Typically, we don't sit down to write with a page number in mind. That's because we'll probably run into one of two problems. Either we'll end up trying to stretch a four-page story into eight pages, or we'll try to compress what could have been a thirty-page story into eight pages. Either way, the result will be a bad eight-page story.

At the beginning of a piece of fiction, you've glimpsed only a fragment of what it might turn out to be. As you explore your way forward, the concept or character or situation or whatever it was that started you down the road of that particular story may turn out to be different from what you first imagined. Most writers I know have had the experience of a work turning into something much larger or smaller than expected. I've started stories that turned into novels, and I've started novels that didn't turn into anything at all.

But there are some clues that can help us predict a story's approximate size-potential ahead of time. Complexity of theme is certainly one factor. Most ideas have multiple facets, and as long as you can keep introducing new facets through which to examine your theme, you can keep extending the story. That also gives you flexibility—you don't have to keep coming up with new facets if you don't want to. The exploration of each facet of the concept, each new dimension of the theme, each fresh complication will bring you to a new exit ramp.

You might find the first of those exits as early as the opening page, but that doesn't mean you have to take it. Then maybe you will have exhausted your exploration of the second facet by page 12. You could end there—unless you've identified a third facet you'd like to explore, which may take you to page 21. A fourth facet may take you to page 35, a fifth to page 58, and so on. If you're wrestling with an idea with enough fresh angles to pursue, you can sustain the story to novel length. But that's optional. You could always take the exit ramps at pages 12, 21, 35, or 58. It's your choice whether to end the story at any one of these natural exit ramps, or to gas up and go further.

For example, maybe you want to explore the idea of fear in a teenage boy:

1. *What if* Bobby is new in town and desperate to be accepted by his peers. But he gets an invitation to join them at the all-night diner downtown after midnight. He's afraid that if he says no, they'll write him off as a loser. But meeting up with them would mean sneaking out at night. He's a good kid, and that goes against his normal behavior.

The decision to go or stay could be the culminating moment of the story, and the story could end as soon as he makes his decision.

But it doesn't have to.

2. *What if* he does sneak out, meets his new pals at the diner, and finds that his buddies have stolen a car to go joy-riding. Does he join them or reject them? That decision could end the story.

But it doesn't have to.

3. So: *what if* he reluctantly goes along? To Bobby's horror, they get chased by cops. Now he's not only afraid of peer-rejection, he's afraid of getting arrested and how that will affect his parents. He's also afraid the driver will crash the stolen car. And maybe the driver does indeed lose control on a curve and roll the car. Bobby is okay, but he suspects not all of his pals are. The story could end with Bobby sitting there in the wreckage waiting to be taken into custody.

But it doesn't have to.

4. *What if* Bobby can't face his predicament, he's terrified that everything in his world has collapsed into rubble, so in absolute panic he scrambles from the car and runs into the dark woods, with the police not far behind. Maybe the story will end with them apprehending the hysterical boy.

But it doesn't have to.

5. *What if* Bobby eludes the police. Will he take shelter in an abandoned house that turns out not to be abandoned after all?

Or will he try to cross a river that turns out to have a stronger current than he expected?

Or will he fall and break his leg?

Or will he escape the police but become hopelessly lost in the forest?

It all depends on what other avenues of fear you want to explore.

The important thing to note here is that, just as there is always an ending in sight, there will also be a new complication in sight. There's no objective criterion for ending a piece of literary fiction. When you arrive at a moment that can serve as a suitable ending, keep in mind that you could just as easily have chosen that moment to introduce a new complication to force the journey onward.

We're teased with this principle all the time in bad

movies. The hero may spend the entire film trying to destroy the monster, and in the end, he does just that. But as the movie takes its leave from us, we get one final shot of some new monster opening an eye. Hello, sequel. In other words, the filmmakers could have continued the story if they'd wished.

A more literary example might be John Updike's novel, *Rabbit, Run*. That novel is complete in itself. But Updike went on to write three more novels about that same character—*Rabbit Redux, Rabbit Is Rich,* and *Rabbit at Rest.* Every ending is also an opportunity for a fresh start.

Shakespeare's *Romeo and Juliet* gives us a perfect example of the multi-faceted approach to extending a story. Yes, everyone knows it's about young love—but it's also more complicated than that. Young love is the core, but Shakespeare takes us through an examination of the many types of complications and issues that arise from young love.

If *R&J* had been a twelve-page story, it would have focused mainly on kids reacting to parental disapproval of their love. Stretch it to 21 pages, and the story has room to work in the problem of the rash and foolhardy choices young people make in the name of love. At 35 pages, we've got space for questions of faithfulness, of true commitment, and whether love is permanent or as transient as the phases of the moon. At 58 pages, we can explore how bystanders get drawn in by the romantic idealism of love among the innocents. At 80 pages we can develop the notion of self-sacrifice in the name of love, and the tragic consequences of breakdowns in communication.

As long as we can keep coming up with new variations on the theme, we can extend any story indefinitely. Shakespeare was no stranger to the principle that a greater complexity of idea required a greater page count. There's a reason *Hamlet* is more than two hours longer than *Macbeth*.

◆ ◆ ◆

Once we start repeating ourselves, however, we've missed our exit. If you've written a great scene exploring one particular aspect of your theme, don't waste the reader's time on additional scenes covering the same territory. It's fine to build upon an earlier aspect, or maybe cover it from a different perspective, but you should avoid basic repetition. Redundancy is not forward movement. Even a scene that's interesting on its own will necessarily be less interesting if placed in tandem with another version of itself. Repetition will always be met by the reader with a diminishing level of interest.

Many of us probably start out thinking we know where our stories are going. That's natural. Sometimes that's just the way a story comes to us—fully formed, as it were, with a clear idea in place for a beginning, middle, and end. That can be a great way to start: *thinking* we know where we're going. It can give us the confidence to push forward.

In my early days, I was often guilty of the mistaken belief that I should know the end of the story before I started writing it. I've since learned the many weaknesses of that approach—predictability not the least among them. But if you do indeed think you know where your story is going, it's unrealistic to try to put that knowledge out of your mind. It's like someone telling you not to think of a donkey. Right now, if I tell you not to think of a donkey, the only thing I can guarantee is that you'll think of a donkey.

So let's say that the preconceived ending of your story is the donkey. Okay, start your story with the donkey in mind. But allow yourself the flexibility to discover along the way that maybe the donkey isn't the optimal ending after all. Maybe the better ending is a Rottweiler, or a grasshopper, or a unicorn. But you'll only discover that if you remain willing to release your grip on the donkey.

◆ ◆ ◆

Most of the great writers from the period of American Romanticism were known for their endings—the stories of Poe and Hawthorne, for example, both of whom were more plot-based than character-based. Melville's *Moby Dick* stuck in many a young reader's imagination because of the culminating clash between the white whale and the whalers, led by Ahab. Those stories were force-fed to me in the educational system, as they likewise may have been force-fed to you.

But those weren't the writers who impressed me the most. When I was ten, the coolest writer I'd yet encountered was O. Henry. You may recall O. Henry's "The Gift of the Magi," in which the young married couple can't afford Christmas presents for each other, so each sells the thing of most value to them to raise money. The loving wife sells her long beautiful hair to a wig maker so she can buy her husband a watch fob to go with the elegant pocket watch he inherited from his family; the husband, meanwhile, sells the watch to buy a fancy set of combs for his wife's long, beautiful hair. Each made a sacrifice and the gifts turned out to be useless. Of course, they still had their love, which was all that mattered. Sappy, certainly. But you can easily see how that kind of story would have to have the ending in place right from the start. That was the case for most of O. Henry's stories, which turned upon some final ironic trick.

But while those stories were impressive to me when I was ten, I'm a little more savvy about irony now. We all are. In fact, as a culture, we're just about irony-ed out. All the plot tricks have been played, and most gimmicks now seem more cheesy than inventive. What used to be called *irony* has come to be called *cheap irony*, a derogatory classification indicating how easy it is to pull the rug out from under a reader with that particular device.

I call such stories punchline fiction. *Punchline* because

everything hinges upon some final gimmick, some twist in the end that the writer has had in mind from the start, the same way a joke-teller knows the punchline when uttering the first line of the joke.

There's nothing wrong with punchline fiction, just as there's nothing wrong with a good joke. But there's a reason there's no "Best Joke" category for the Pulitzer Prize. Some literary forms are simply more sophisticated than others. Punchline fiction is almost always linear, plot-driven fiction of minimal depth. There are books I've returned to multiple times in my life, like *The Great Gatsby* and William Kennedy's *Ironweed,* each of which I've read at least half a dozen times; and I always seem to appreciate something in the work that I missed the previous times. But never in my life, after hearing a great joke, have I asked the joke-teller to tell it to me again. Jokes don't gain depth or power upon multiple hearings. A good work of fiction is like a deep well; punchline fiction is a puddle drying in the sun. Puddles can be fun to splash around in, but they can't provide the long-term nourishment one can draw from a well.

But good wells are hard to dig. And you won't know ahead of time if you'll ever hit water. I imagine every writer has labored over a multitude of dry holes. Art always goes hand in hand with frustration and self-doubt.

Formula writing is far easier. The majority of fiction writers who make a minor living writing do so by cranking out formula fiction. You don't need teachers to teach you that kind of writing, especially in the romance novel field, which is the market leader. Just ask the publisher for a set of guidelines and get to work. Connect all the dots they tell you to connect and you'll have a completed book. But that isn't a very imaginative approach to writing fiction. The only talent it requires is the ability to follow instructions.

If you want the big bucks, head for Hollywood. When I edited a literary journal, I used to get regular submissions from a Hollywood writer who had literary aspirations. He never came close to getting anything published, because his fiction was both implausible and surprisingly bland. Yet he has written several box-office hits and a string of successful television shows. He's a master of the high-concept fantasy plot.

I'm not suggesting everyone should try to be the next F. Scott Fitzgerald—though that's not a bad aspiration. I've chosen the literary side of the fence myself, and I can prove it by the fact that I don't own a yacht. And I do blatantly proselytize for the yachtless path. Samuel Beckett counseled us wisely when he pointed out that all our literary efforts were doomed to failure. But our goal, he said, should always be to *fail better.*

There's an archery analogy that might help me clarify what I think a good failure is all about. A simple punchline story, one in which you've made a beeline to the ending that you had in mind all along, is the equivalent of hitting the target dead center with your arrow, but from a distance of four feet. If hitting the target dead center every time is all that matters to you, then limiting your shots to the four-foot range makes sense. You can always score a bullseye from that distance. Just don't expect to impress anyone. I have more interest in the arrow that just nicks one of the outer rings of the target, if that arrow has been fired from three hundred feet away. The ambitious shot from greater distance is more impressive to me, even though it might not hit the bullseye.

At that distance, of course, you might miss the target altogether. But every now and then, you might land one dead center, and that's something to be proud of. In terms of a personal literary heritage, fifty perfect hits from right in front of the target wouldn't mean as much to me as one bullseye from a football field away. Dare to be ambitious in your work.

Now back to our guiding metaphor, the road trip. Let's keep in mind that, even though there may be some dips and plateaus along the way, the overall direction is uphill. That's not just because writing is hard work. It's uphill because of what we call the *rising action line.*

The first time I heard that term, probably in a high school English class, I'm sure I had no idea what rising action meant. Maybe you've got some confusion on that point, too. Think of it like sitting in a roller coaster at the beginning of the ride. You're slowly being pulled uphill toward the scary drop. But as you're being tugged along at this slow, steady pace, something happens to you. Maybe your heart begins to beat a little faster. Maybe beads of sweat pop out on your forehead. Maybe your grip tightens on the safety bar. Maybe you unconsciously hold your breath. Maybe you even start mumbling curses to yourself for getting on the ride in the first place. But however the tension manifests itself, there is a growing sense of tension as you anticipate reaching that crest, because that's the climactic moment when the thrill will intensify, and you can see it coming. That's rising action: the on-track movement through increasing tensions until finally something has to give. The power and energy that accumulates during the long uphill pull is what propels the story forward for the rest of the ride.

So if you're having trouble finding an exit ramp for your story, ask yourself if the story is on track in the first place. Maybe you got on the wrong ride. Maybe instead of the roller coaster—that wild up-and-down grown-up ride that stays on track—you got on one of the kiddie rides instead. Maybe you boarded the bumper cars, a ride with no sense of direction at all, no rising action, just one meaningless flatland collision after another, without any consequences being carried forward. If your story gets stuck on the bumper car ride, you'll never find your exit because there isn't one. There's no cause and effect, only random action. When that ride is over, the cars are simply abandoned where they sit, having arrived nowhere.

While we're at the carnival, I'll mention another writerly ride to avoid: the merry-go-round. Sure, it has ups and downs, but it doesn't really go anywhere. The end will be uneventful.

The ferris wheel has the same problem. Though it appears to have rising action, the characters cycle through the same point over and over and never undergo any kind of dynamic change.

The tilt-a-whirl might work for a short story because it has lots of unpredictable movement in a confined space. But don't try to write a tilt-a-whirl novel. You'll just get dizzy, and the ending will leave you queasy and confused.

The reason I stress the importance of getting on the right ride is that every semester I have students who turn in stories with endings that just don't work. Sometimes the problem is with the ending itself—some action may be forced or some emotional or psychological leap has been made that's false to the character or situation.

But more often than not, there's absolutely nothing wrong with the ending except for the fact that it doesn't work. That might sound contradictory, but often the reason an ending doesn't work has little to do with the ending itself. The ending might be theoretically fine. The problem might come from somewhere in the beginning or middle of a story. The fact is, nearly any ending can work if it's set up properly. Sometimes potentially great endings simply aren't supported or justified by what preceded them.

So if an editor or some early readers tell you that your ending doesn't work, remember that they may be identifying a symptom, not a root cause. If the ending doesn't work, but you feel in your bones that it's right, then go back to the story and figure out what needs to be changed along the way to justify that ending.

If you're given a beautiful and expensive pair of shoes that don't fit, they don't belong on your feet. Likewise, if your ending doesn't fit, it doesn't belong on the story as it exists so far. Luckily, it's easier to reshape a story than to reshape our feet.

But let's say your ending doesn't work because, well, it's a bad ending, and you know it. That's not uncommon, but it's still frustrating. Maybe you've tried to end the story too soon, and the real ending lies further along the track. Maybe you've overshot the ending without realizing it.

There are two ways to make the mistake of overshooting your ending. The first involves the gangly proposition of having a story with two endings. The first might come unnoticed on, say, page 17 and the second on page 20. That's often the result of a split focus in the story, when the main story arc completes itself without the writer realizing it because of a misplaced preoccupation with a secondary character whom the writer may mistakenly believe the story is about. You have to know whose story it is—which character the story is truly about—before you can recognize the completion of the main story arc.

That might seem like a ridiculous mistake to make. Surely, we always know which character is the centerpiece. But sometimes that's a discovery to which we're slow to awaken. In early drafts, we may think one character is the heart of the piece, only to realize in draft number four that she's really just a catalyst for another character's epiphany. If one character remains static while another undergoes dynamic change, the dynamic character is the one the story is about, regardless how much more page space may have been devoted to the static character. The character who changes is the one who matters, and once that character's story arc is completed, you need to get out.

The other way to overshoot an ending doesn't involve a split focus; instead, the action simply fizzles to a non-ending after the real ending had already taken place. We end up wallowing in the aftermath.

I learned about overshooting endings with my first published story. It was, I'm now chagrined to say, a

Poe-like tale of madness in which a disgraced diamond cutter tries to prove his expertise by removing the top of his own skull, and it appeared in a now-defunct literary magazine. I was delighted with the publication—the magazine even commissioned artwork to go with it. But there was a problem. When the story appeared in print, the last page of the manuscript was inadvertently left off. I was horrified and they were apologetic. But then I realized something: the story was better without the last page. All that had been lost was an unnecessary explanation to the reader, as if I were telling a five-year-old the moral of a fairy tale.

From then on I made a conscious effort to patrol my endings to make sure I didn't slip back into the old mode of supplying unnecessary conclusions. It's enough to point a direction at the end of a story and let the reader follow it out in his or her own imagination. The impulse to sum up is the impulse to assume ignorance on the part of the reader, and the reader deserves more respect than that. Condescension is fine if you're talking to preschoolers, who might need their little morality tales explained to them. But adults prefer to put the pieces together themselves and draw their own conclusions.

I'm not here to tell you what kind of approach to take to your endings, but I will tell you that there are many workable variations. In some stories the narrative may end by jumping ahead to some relevant point in the future, or to the point from which the teller is telling the tale. Sometimes the writer closes on a metaphorical action or image. Sometimes we're left with a final visual scene of the characters simply doing something together, as so often happens in film. Sometimes a defining dramatic act or line can bring a story to a close. On rare occasion a story might even end on a note of philosophical mystery, as in "The Lady or the Tiger" by Frank Stockton. There are doubtless many other tactics for taking one's leave of a story.

But regardless of what type of ending you opt for, an

ending is always available to you at a moment's notice. When you feel your story is losing momentum and you just can't keep it chugging up that rising action line, all you have to do is take stock of the ground you've covered and make an intuitive choice that's somehow a culmination of whatever tensions the story has established so far. Trust your intuition.

Intuition is key. Formula fiction can be assembled by following a set of instructions, but not literary fiction. We aren't engaged in a mechanical execution of a builder's plan. We aren't just filling in blanks or connecting predetermined plot points, we're engaged in a process of discovery. Discovery calls for the subjectivity only a human sensibility can bring to the equation. An artistic sensibility.

So first we identify the potential stopping point, then we assess what got us there, and then we contemplate what action or image will best convey the totality of the experience. The ending appropriate on page twelve won't be the ending that's most appropriate on page 21, and that won't be the right ending for page 35 or page 58. But there's always an appropriate ending ready for the imagining at any point in a well-constructed story. Whenever you want to bring the journey to a close, you can. Maybe that means building your own exit ramp in the middle of a big city or out someplace in the middle of nowhere. But even in the middle of nowhere, a story can always end perfectly.

8

THE EDITOR'S VIEW

What's Wrong with This Picture?

For those relatively new to the path, I recommend becoming part of a writing group. It's helpful to have a dedicated community of readers who aren't family members look at your work and tell you honestly what they think. They're on the same path you are, and their concern is the same as yours—improvement. You'll also learn as much by critiquing their work as you will from their critiquing yours. Learning to spot strengths and weaknesses is the key to revision.

Because we're human and therefore both blessed and cursed with ego, it's far easier to apply our critical lens to someone else's work than to our own. Looking outward is far easier than looking inward; being honest with others is less painful than being honest with ourselves. That's because we can find the flaw in someone else's work without running the risk of damaging our own sense of self-worth. Because our ego is at stake, it's tough to look at our own work and pronounce it unworthy.

That's the way it has to be. If ego didn't first lie to us and tell us our crappy work was wonderful, we'd never get a first draft written. And the truth is, just about all fine writing starts out with some degree of crappy-ness to it. If our critical lenses were fully functional from the moment we put the first word on the page, we'd all freeze up in perpetual writer's block. The balance we must learn to strike is first to cocoon ourselves in the delusion that what we're writing is worthwhile; then we need to break through that cocoon and revise the work into what it truly ought to be. So our first psychological task is to give ourselves permission to fail.

I once saw the first draft of Ken Kesey's novel, *One Flew Over the Cuckoo's Nest*, which is one of my favorite books. The opening chapter was virtually unreadable. Poorly paced, unfocused, clumsily written, and dull. But if Kesey hadn't written that tortured early version, he could never have reached the amazing final one.

If literary giants can botch things, we shouldn't expect our own work to emerge without missteps. T. S. Eliot once wrote a poem called "He Do the Police in Different Voices" which changed the landscape of modern poetry. But we don't know it by that title. Eliot took the advice of his friend, Ezra Pound, who told him the title was stupid, and that he should call it "The Waste Land" instead.

Pound himself had a famous poem called "In the Station of the Metro" that was only two lines long: *The apparition of these faces in the crowd: / Petals on a wet, black bough.* The original draft was thirty lines long.

Keep in mind that revision is a privilege, not a chore. One of the great blessings of our craft is that we can tinker with a story until we get it right. Still, I've known many beginners who hated getting reader feedback, regarding all criticism as a slap in the face, an invalidation of the work they'd already done. To revise was to admit to their flaws. Consequently, they approached revision with a sense of resistance, and even defeat.

But revision isn't a form of punishment for your mistakes, and it doesn't have to be a major undertaking. Don't think of revision as tossing a grenade into the story and blowing everything apart. Think of it instead as a surgical procedure in which you go back into the text and make the slightest adjustments possible to fix things. If you've taken care with your previous draft and not run headlong into entirely wrong directions, most remaining problems can be resolved by tiny touches here and there, a new sentence or phrase, a few swapped words, a few judicious cuttings. Placing exactly the right new phrase in exactly the right spot can have the effect of a train signalman pulling a single lever that switches the entire train onto a different track, sending it to its proper destination.

Your readers don't have to be as insightful as Ezra Pound. For now, they may be people you know, but eventually they'll be strangers, people you may never meet, people who picked up your work and, for reasons entirely their own, decided not to put it down. Here's what you need to know about those anonymous readers: they'll be the toughest critics you'll ever encounter. That's because they know what they like; if you bore them, they'll know it. When it comes to perceptivity, those readers will scrutinize your manuscript like Sherlock Holmes examining a crime scene. Whatever clue you leave that might suggest you aren't in full control of your material, those readers will see. Don't for an instant let yourself believe that no one will notice the problems. Even the smallest error can blow your credibility. Don't ever give your readers cause to doubt you.

So how do we head off that doubt and keep the readers reading? The answer is simple: you need to train yourself to be the first unbiased reader. You need to become Sherlock Holmes before any other reader gets a chance to play that role. Treat your rough draft as a crime scene—which for some of us may not be much of a stretch—and consider yourself to be the first investigator to take a really close look at it.

But what stumbles should you be looking for in your sleuthing? The same things editors are likely to notice.

Here are twenty-three common problems which you can easily fix in the revision process:

1

Bullshit in the language. We all have those phrases we fall in love with in our writing, but sometimes they're just too puffed up, too phony, too falsely poetic to deserve a place in the manuscript. If you've ever heard the writerly advice to "kill your darlings," such unseemly ornamentation is what the phrase refers to. Yes, elevated language can be lovely, but not if it intrudes, not if it draws attention away from the narrative and shines a self-conscious, self-congratulatory light on the author. Any line that says, "Hey, look what a great writer I am!" is actually accomplishing the opposite of what you want it to. Such lines don't stand out as poetic moments, they stand out as little Frankenstein monsters, and you should go after them with torches and pitchforks.

That doesn't mean you can't sometimes arrive at beautiful turns of phrase and legitimately poetic passages. But those moments shouldn't be forced or incongruous to the character, emotional situation, or mood. They have to arise naturally from the voice of the character or from the context.

Also, you should never try to show off your vocabulary by using obscure phrases to describe common things. The novelist Bynum Shaw told me that the most embarrassing passage in his entire body of work was a phrase he used to describe two people arguing and waving their arms as they talked. He wrote that they were engaged in "gesticulating logomachy." Don't do that. It breaks the spell of the narrative and draws attention to the writer.

2

Don't pad your sentences, either. Any time you write a sentence that should take only a few words, you could easily pile on the flab to say the same thing in a more roundabout way. Again, I'll blame our educational system, which inadvertently trained us to pad our sentences as a means of academic survival. How many times did we have some English assignment that was supposed to be ten pages long, and we had only four pages worth of ideas? The solution of course was to expand every ten-word thought to twenty-five words or more. In high school that tactic probably made you look smart, but not anymore. Fiction calls for a different mindset. If a word can be cut out, cut it out.

Here's a useful exercise. First, read one of your stories or chapters aloud and time it. Then pretend that you have to give a public reading of that piece in a time slot that requires cutting a quarter of the material. Let's say it's twenty minutes long and you have the stage for only fifteen minutes. Then go through the manuscript and remove five minutes of the least essential material. For the final draft, you may put some of it back, but I think you'll be amazed at how much dead weight your story can shed without harm—and the pace will be improved in the process.

3

Personification isn't as cool as you thought it was in junior high. In literary terms, it's called the *pathetic fallacy*. Nature has many grand traits, but being human isn't one of them. So resist the urge to have the sun smile down at Elmo. Don't let those tree branches beckon Enid into the forest.

Also, avoid having parts acting independently of the whole. It tends to make the work too self-conscious and sometimes laughable. If a character's feet walk up the steps, we may wonder what happened to the rest of him. I saw a passage once in which a character "rolled his eyes around the room," which was unintentionally funny and grotesque. There might be occasional moments when such disembodiments are called for, but those should be the rare exceptions.

4

If your story is set in the real world, make sure it passes the real-world test. Too many times I see writers write about things involving the court system, police procedures, medical issues, or business transactions—to name but a few examples—when it's clear they know no more about the reality of their subject than what they've picked up from television. Any time you put a character in a situation that falls outside your own daily experience, you have an obligation to do the research so the procedures will be authentic. I had a writing teacher once who told me that after one of his novels was published he got a flood of letters about a mistake he'd made—having two streets in Baltimore intersect that, in reality, never do. Things like that matter to readers. Such missteps can leave the reader feeling betrayed, because you will have destroyed the illusion of reality.

Apply reality checks to everyday moments. Here's a mistake I came across recently: a woman took a package of barbecue pork from the freezer and took a moment to enjoy the aroma. But frozen food doesn't give off an aroma.

Light and dark often present problems as well. Countless times I've read descriptions of two characters standing together in the pitch dark on a moonless night, only to have one of them be captivated by the other's striking blue eyes. Nope, not gonna happen. If you make the setting dark, you can't include details that would be visible only in the light.

5

You've heard that showing is usually preferable to telling. Here's a corollary: Don't tell what you show. Often I see exchanges like this: *Harry wanted Eddie to get out of the way. "Get out of my way, Eddie," he said.* Things like that should be left in the Department of Redundancy Department.

6

Avoid hyperbole because the world will come to an end if you don't. Her eyes don't have to burn like a million stars. Mom doesn't have to look with blood-curdling horror at the cookie crumbs Junior left on the counter. The common mistake, it seems, is to think that by cranking up the volume, so to speak, the material becomes more powerful. But the opposite is the case; overstatement damages the plausibility of the moment, and so weakens the impact. Keep in mind that a quietly closed door can be far more powerful than a slammed one. Anything that seems inappropriately over-the-top can drain power from a story. If a character cries six times in a twelve-page story, the tears will become less and less meaningful. By the sixth time, they may even seem ridiculous.

7

Check for thematic unity. The writer/teacher John Gardner believed that every work of literature should have a governing metaphor. That's similar to T. S. Eliot's claim that every good literary work should have an objective correlative. What they're both calling for is some action or image to provide the symbolic framework for the story—some symbol or metaphor that encapsulates what the story is about at its core. If you have such a guiding image in mind, you can use it to keep yourself on the right thematic track. If a scene you're writing has nothing to do with your theme, then you'll know you may be veering off in a wrong direction.

8

Central characters can exhibit all kinds of emotions, but self-pity is the least attractive, and readers tend to have little patience for such whiners. After all, if a character feels sorry for himself or herself, readers don't have to. Self-pity can work for a secondary character, especially one we aren't supposed to like or one we're to regard as ridiculous. You can use self-pity as a brief starting point for a main character, but don't let the character wallow there for too long.

9

Remember that verbs carry the real freight of good writing, not adjectives and certainly not adverbs. In fiction, one or two adverbs per page is plenty. Part of the problem is that adverbs are often superfluous. *"I hate you!" John screamed angrily.* Well, what other way is there to scream such a line? The adverb adds nothing to the line, which tells the reader that you aren't in touch with your own material. If the parts of speech are the ingredients in a banana split, verbs are the ice cream, nouns are the bananas, adjectives are the syrupy toppings, prepositions are the nuts and sprinkles. Adverbs are paprika. Use *sparingly*, if at all.

But not every action verb is holy. Go easy on the fancy dialogue tags. Yes, I know they encouraged us to be inventive with them back in eighth grade, but that was just to show us the possibilities. In some situations, it's okay to tag your dialogue with expressive verbs, but more often than not, they just sound clunky. *"Oh!" Mary uttered. "Oh," Mary ejaculated. "Oh!" Mary enunciated. "Oh!" Mary orated. ""Oh!" Mary expounded. "Oh!" Mary declaimed.* There are dozens of possible dialogue tags out there—lines may be cried, laughed, dictated, raged, barked, bawled, jabbered, howled, shrieked, retorted, blurted, groaned, lilted, joked, sniveled, lamented, insisted, giggled, questioned, preached, roared, whined, groveled, pleaded, exclaimed, empathized, stammered, and who knows what else. But if you keep decorating your dialogue with these off-beat tags, the tags will become a distraction to the reader. Ninety percent of the time, a simple *said* or *asked* will do. And even those should be used only when the identity of the speaker isn't obvious. True, *said* is probably the most neutral and boring of all tags, but most of the time it's the very invisibility of the word that makes it so useful. An invisible tag never distracts the reader.

10

Avoid repeating distinctive words. An editor at Doubleday once made me change a word on page 235 because I'd used it once before on page 27. Even with a two-hundred page separation, he felt the repetition was too noticeable because the word was too distinctive.

11

Tension should be ever-present. Imagine the following story:

A man is out hunting in the woods when a sudden storm blows in. He spots an empty rental cabin with an open front door, so he seeks shelter inside. His coat is soaked from the rain, so he takes it off and looks around for a place to hang it, then drapes it over a chair. Then he realizes he's hungry and begins rummaging through the cabin for food. He's about to check the pantry when the lights go out because of the storm. He tries to search for the fuse box, but before he finds it, the lights come back on. He sits down on the ratty sofa to rest, and a bear comes out of the pantry and kills him.

That's a bad story. It has a climax, but no rising action to take us there, and no tension to generate momentum. If we were to draw this story structure on a graph, the story would be a flat line across the bottom until the emergence of the bear, and then the graph would show a vertical spike. That's unsatisfying storytelling structure.

But imagine the same story if we knew from the start there was a bear in the pantry. Then every mundane action would suddenly take on significance. When he enters the cabin, we'd know the risk involved. When he takes off his coat, we'd be fearful he might hang it in the pantry, and feel relief when he drapes it over a chair. When he searches for food, we'd be fearful he might look inside the pantry, and feel relief when the blackout interrupts his progress. When he searches in the dark for the fuse box, we'd be fearful that he'd check for it in the pantry, and feel relief when the lights come back on. Fear, relief, fear, relief, fear, relief—story tension building with every rise and fall of possibility.

If the reader is made immediately aware of the bear in the pantry, every action will contain powerful potential—life and death potential, in this particular case. As long as that tension continues to build, the bear never even needs to come out of the pantry for the story to succeed.

So keep this imaginary bear in mind as you write your stories. At every moment, from page one forward, ask yourself if the reader knows about the bear in the pantry. If there's no bear in the pantry from the beginning, you haven't found your true opening yet.

12

Product placement does not add realism to a story. Brand names can be distracting in a manuscript, and sooner or later they'll become obscure. If someone uses *Ipana* in a story, few readers will know what it is—even though it was once one of the country's top-selling brands of toothpaste. Something that's a national fad today will be forgotten trivia a few years down the road. And the same goes for pop culture references. Just because you watched a TV show religiously as a child, or loved a particular song, or read a particular book, that doesn't mean your readers did, so insider references won't carry any meaning.

13

Don't hide behind an obscure prose style or a bizarre approach. There are plenty of legitimate experimental writers—people like Cris Mazza, Michael Martone,

Aimee Bender, Robert Coover, Donald Barthelme, and, on occasion, Jennifer Egan, among hordes of others—who have brought freshness to the literary scene. But there are plenty of lesser talents out there, too, who dilute the public's impression of what experimental fiction is all about. Often they're writers who have over-committed themselves to self-expression at the expense of communication. Never let yourself abandon the first duty of art, which is to communicate.

When I was a literary editor, I once received a packet of "fictions" from someone who billed himself as an avant-garde writer. He was not an unknown figure on the experimental literary scene, and in fact I'd published some of his earlier oddities. But this submission was a collection of geometric shapes. No sentences, no words, just shapes. Squares, octagons, triangles, ovals. He said each one was a piece of experimental fiction, and that the reader was to stare at the shape until a story came to mind. For me, that batch of drawings was a failed literary experiment because it shifted the entire workload from writer to reader.

Now, geometry-as-fiction is probably an extreme case by any standard. Maybe he was branching into a different field, becoming more of a conceptual artist than a writer. Maybe we have no name for what he was doing. But I suspect he wasn't helping the cause of the avant-garde with experiments like that one, which could only open the door to all the fakes out there trying to pass off inadequacy as cutting-edge experimentalism.

There's no substitute for the discipline and capacity for hard work that it takes to sit down and write. Don't ever let laziness creep into your work under the guise of experimentalism. Real experimentalism is as difficult to do well as any other literary form, and anything less than your best effort is a betrayal of the art, no matter how many people might say they like it. Plenty of insecure people said they liked the Emperor's new clothes, but they were all lying.

14

Don't confuse complication with climax. I see far too many inexperienced writers mistake a complication for the culmination of the action. Generally speaking, a story should not end with a car crash. A story should not end with the wife walking in on her husband having an affair. A story should not end with the collapse of a building full of people. Readers might be somewhat interested in events, but they're more interested in how characters process those events. Aftermath of crisis is what matters, not the crisis itself.

15

Never take a condescending approach to writing a character. Condescension reduces characters to cartoons. You should be creating people, not targets. Write your characters with a parental sense of forgiveness. Even your most despicable character should be someone who, under a different set of circumstances, could easily have been you or someone you love.

16

Keep in mind that there should always be tension between what the character wants and what the character needs. The alcoholic wants a drink but needs to stop drinking. The thief wants to rob the bank but needs to go straight. The husband wants to have an affair but needs to remain faithful. The athlete wants to win the big game but needs to pay more attention to his family. The anorexic wants to lose weight but needs to eat better. The gap between the want and the need will drive the narrative forward.

17

Reading should be a full sensory experience for the reader. Because we tend to hammer home the "show, don't tell" advice, it's easy to forget that showing isn't enough. Yes, we should always give the reader a firm grounding in the visual dimension of the story, but we shouldn't neglect the other senses. Put smells into your fiction, and tastes, and textures, and sounds. Round out the sensory experience and your fiction will better capture the world. The more complete the sensory experience, the deeper the material will take root in the reader's memory.

18

Pace keeps a story alive, and there are two ways to ruin the pace of a story—going too slow, or going too fast. Obviously, the problem with going too slow is that you'll bore the reader. But there's an equal danger in speeding through things too quickly. The reader needs a chance to become immersed in the experience—to live through it with the characters. A speeding narrative tends to skim the surface, providing little more than a summary of events. I once read the autobiography of Buffalo Bill, and I was amazed at the breakneck pace he set. He might join the Pony Express, ride eight hundred miles, escape a band of outlaws, talk his way past a Sioux war party, and kill a few renegades from another tribe, all on a single page. But Buffalo Bill was never about depth, he was about flash and dazzle—showmanship, rather than literature. There's nothing wrong with a little showmanship, but temper it with the character's inner life. If Buffalo Bill tries to run off with your story, tie a couple of cinder blocks to his feet and give him something to think about.

19

Characters are often defined by the choices they make. Keep in mind that when you give any character a choice, it shouldn't be between good or evil, right or wrong. That's not a real choice because there's no dilemma involved. No one with a functioning brain would intentionally choose poorly. The choice needs to be clouded by competing factors, creating a decision between two irreconcilable goods or between two competing evils. Each choice must carry its own combination of losses and gains, and the character must always believe he or she is making the proper call.

For example, a man who shoots a child's dog is a villain—unless the dog is rabid, in which case the man is a hero. But what if the man only suspects the dog might be rabid? Then there's a difficult choice to make that has nothing to do with being a hero or a villain. Cartoon characters can be heroes or villains, but literature is built upon flesh and blood—which means it depends upon people who have tough choices to make.

20

This may seem obvious, but keep track of time and space. I often see passages in student work in which characters in a restaurant order drinks or dinners, and after two lines of dialogue, the waitress reappears at the table with the margaritas or hamburgers. Two lines of dialogue later, the drinks have been downed or the hamburgers finished and the characters are ready to pay the check. Page time does not pass at the same rate as writing time. Even though it took you all morning to write the page, only thirty seconds have passed for the characters. Keep yourself plugged into their time frame.

21

Be consistent with your point of view. If the story is told through Mary's perspective, don't slip for a line or two into John's innermost thoughts. This is one of the most common mistakes I see.

22

What happens *below* the surface is far more important than what happens *on* the surface. Stories are about experience, not events. So ask yourself what your story is about. If the answer is external—*It's about a guy who wins the lottery*—you're probably writing a superficial and forgettable story. If your answer is internal—*It's about a guy who struggles to comprehend the meaning of value in his life after winning the lottery*—then you have a chance of writing something that endures, something that might connect with the people who read it. That's the goal, after all—to write something that connects us all, and thereby enlarges the world we share.

23

Sweat the small stuff. All fine writing is built upon what William Blake called the "minute particulars." That means that grammar, syntax, punctuation, and style all matter. Poor command of the basic elements of writing will signal to an editor that you aren't in control of your craft. The assumption then becomes that anything you may do right is accidental.

So learn how to use commas. That's crucial. Not one student writer in five knows the ins and outs of proper comma usage. Set yourself apart by using commas correctly.

Beyond that, there are two other punctuation pitfalls to be concerned with—semicolons and exclamation points. Both tend to be overused. I've seen writers use ten semicolons per page, when ten would probably be enough for a three-hundred-page novel. Inexperienced writers seem to think the semicolon gives their work more sophistication, since it's a rarefied form. When in doubt, they toss in a semicolon. But that just draws attention to the writer and comes across as an affectation. Real sophistication lies more in the simple mastery of the comma than in an ostentatious display of semicolons.

As for exclamation points, avoid them! Such writerly shouting is unseemly! The exclamation point represents an extreme, and can seem comical if overused! Save it for rare outbursts! Unless you're writing for preschoolers, stick to periods!

A WRITER'S CHECKLIST

Twenty Tee-Shirt-Worthy Aphorisms on Writing

With the possible exceptions of the Gettysburg Address and Hamlet's "To be or not to be" speech, all the smart or useful passages I've encountered in literature, *belle-lettres*, or philosophy have had one thing in common: extreme brevity. If you can't fit it on a tee-shirt, you probably haven't boiled it down enough. So here are twenty things I believe to be true about writing fiction. Some of it I've already brought up in earlier chapters, but I've reintroduced it here not because I want to stretch my page count, as I used to do in college lit papers, but because certain concepts are important enough to bear repeating. Besides, sometimes saying something a different way can make it more understandable. In keeping with my goal of brevity, I've limited each point to three words. Then, of course, I've beaten each point to death with a long-winded elaboration, since that is, after all, what teachers do.

1
Character Needs Backstory

Backstory provides the context for understanding who a character truly is. Characters without individual backstories—either implicit or explicit—are often just stick figures. Types. But once you've given them a context, they start to emerge from the shadows and take on real identities.

Imagine: five teenagers witness a car crash. What do they do? If they have no backstories, maybe they just stare at the wreckage. After all, what else can they do if they're just a group of interchangeable teenagers. Without backstories, there can be no individuality—and that means that you, as the author, have no basis upon which to determine their five different responses. Backstory is what makes each character unique, and it's what triggers individual actions.

So the first teenager—the one who lost her parents in a similar wreck—begins to shake so hard she has to steady herself against a light pole. The second, who has spent too much of his life playing race-track video games and has lost empathy for real-life versions of his fantasy world, breaks into nervous laughter, because he isn't sure what reaction is appropriate. The third—the one who thinks she recognizes the car—calls her friend to make sure he's all right. The fourth—that straight-A student who is always so organized—calls for an ambulance. The fifth—the one who has been thinking about joining the army because he fears that, deep down, he might be a coward—rushes to the wreck to help the injured. That's five different responses, each response determined by how the minute particulars of life have shaped each character in different ways.

That doesn't mean we need to know entire life histories. Backstory should be selective, not comprehensive. Nothing from a character's past belongs in a story unless it contributes directly to our understanding of something the character is doing in the present. That's where focus comes in. When you're providing us with backstory details, your focus mustn't stray from the relevant incidents of the past. If there are no dogs in the story's present line of action, we probably don't need to know that a character was bitten by a chihuahua when she was ten. But if that chihuahua left scars on her face that she continues to feel self-conscious about, then there's a reason to give us that piece of backstory. Characters without backstory are often names without an identity, place-cards in an empty banquet hall.

2
Traumas Echo Forward

This is an important truth about backstory. Every choice you make about a character's past is a rock you're dropping into the pond of the story. The size of the rock will vary, and the bigger the rock, the larger the ripple effect will be in the life of the character.

If George had an allergic reaction to ice cream when he was a child, that's probably just a pebble in the pond, and maybe it explains why he doesn't order ice cream when he's on his date with Heloise. No big deal. But if George had been kidnapped by psychopaths when he was a child and tortured with a soldering iron for three days before being rescued in a bloody shootout, that's a boulder dropped into the pond, and the ripples from that will reach every shore of his consciousness, profoundly affecting how he interacts with everyone in the present world of his story. Maybe it ruins his shot at a future with Heloise because her Southern accent reminds him of that painful episode. Such traumas never stay in the past; they always intrude in the character's hopes and dreams.

3
Premise Is Expendable

Maybe you get this great idea, this magnificent *What if?* that starts the ball rolling. That's terrific. But maybe as the story develops, you discover other interesting and productive directions that ultimately negate the initial premise. Don't feel bound by your original idea. Stories should grow organically, and whatever grows should be nurtured. Maybe you thought you planted a pumpkin and an oak tree grew instead. Don't grumble about the loss of the pumpkin, embrace the oak tree. Don't try to carve the oak tree into that jack-o'-lantern you first had in mind. The job of the premise is to get you writing. After that, your only allegiance should be to the story as you discover it.

4
It's Never Easy

I'm often asked if the longer one works at writing, the easier it will get. No. Sorry. The work will get better, but not easier. That's why so few people become successful writers—as soon as they realize the kind of focus and attention to detail and hard work it always requires, they quit.

Of course, it's fine for people to pursue writing as a fun recreational activity, but that's not the same as pursuing it as an art form. It's one thing to have fun playing touch football in your back yard, but it's another thing entirely to play in the NFL. The work is always hardest at the top of any field.

You're getting better now because you're making demands upon yourself. As soon as you stop making those demands and start coasting, you're dead as an artist. Then all you can do is keep writing some version of the same book over and over. I know plenty of writers who have done just that. They're usually the ones who have become brand names. Redundancy is, in fact, the most common way to become a brand name, because it's something big-time publishers encourage. They want to position you in the marketplace and have their advertising dollars build a steady clientele, so naturally they're more interested in predictability from you than in original artistic creation.

They're not wrong for doing that—publishers have no choice but to view writing as a commodity in a profit-driven business. Just be aware of what signing the big contract will likely mean. If some New York publishing house brings out your gritty courtroom drama and it's a great financial success, the last thing in the world they'll want you to do next is try your hand at science fiction, or a western, or a children's book. They'll want another gritty courtroom drama. If that's what you truly want to write, great. Maybe you can make each successive courtroom drama more complex, more literary than the last. Maybe you can stretch the boundaries of the genre and use it as a vehicle for plumbing greater depths of the human experience. But I hope you won't do it solely for the money, cranking out multiple versions of the same book over and over, as your version of Perry Mason wins case after case in the same predictable manner. If you want to make a mark as an artist, write whatever kind of book represents the most interesting challenge for you. Growth as an artist comes through exploration, not repetition.

5
Story Before Setting

Many inexperienced writers make the mistake of giving us a lot of details about setting before launching into the story. That's runway building, a risky tactic I've mentioned before, and it's perhaps the most common stumble I encounter in student work. Most of us have a natural tendency to start by describing the locale—as if we're staging a play at which the audience has arrived early enough to read over the program notes before the curtain rises on the action.

Skip the runway; start the story in midair. Sure, we need description and exposition, but most of that can and should be worked into the action. If you lump it all together into a cumbersome block at the opening, the reader may not make it to wherever it is you've actually started the story. Readers are notorious for skipping over the static descriptive parts to get to dialogue and action. Worse yet, those readers who do read your long-winded introductory passages might find themselves bored enough to put down the story and go do something else. Readers invest their interest in the predicaments of characters, not in locales, so hook us first on an intriguing situation. Don't leave the static descriptive material out, just break it into palatable nuggets and pass it along to us after our interest has already been engaged.

6
Experience, Not Events

I've covered this before, but it's important enough to bear repeating. Stories are not about what happens, they are about the people to whom things happen. What happens is merely the surface level, and literature is about what's below the surface. Your story should lead us to an understanding of why and how the events of the narrative have affected the character internally. An event is a catalyst for experience, for some inner directional change in the character. The event isn't the reason for the story to exist, the new moment of awareness is. Granted, the two will be linked; but ultimately the inner change in character matters more than any external change in circumstance. Stories turn on the epiphany, the moment of new awareness. Usually the epiphany is what makes the main character dynamic, rather than static.

But there's also such a thing as the *reader epiphany,* in which the reader realizes in the end that the character is too oblivious, weak, or stubborn to change. Then it's the reader who has been brought to a new awareness of the character's true nature.

7
Show, Don't Tell

I have to include this one or I'll lose my union card as a writing teacher. It's the one piece of advice we all give at every level, so you've probably encountered it before. It's our national anthem—and like that other anthem, it raises the crucial question, *Oh, say, can you see...?*

Why should seeing be the goal? Because people remember what they've seen more effectively than what they've been told. Abstractions, ideas, and information all evaporate more quickly from the mind than do concrete images—that's why one picture is worth a thousand words.

If the reader can see the action in his or her own imagination, the image will enter into memory as a lived experience. In order for the reader to live the experience, you have to create a moment-by-moment sensory reality. In fact, that reality should unfold in even smaller increments: micro-moment by micro-moment.

Creating the micro-moment experience is some of the hardest work of fiction, but it also pays the highest dividend. The entire story of *Moby Dick* could be told in just a few pages, but that wouldn't really give us the experience of the voyage.

So be careful about just having your characters sit around musing about things. The philosophy behind those musings might be profound, but profundity doesn't do you much good unless you've packaged it in an engaging and memorable way, and that requires conjuring up an action or image within which to house your ideas.

8
Telling's Okay Too

Yes, it's usually better to show than to tell, but let's not go overboard. Sometimes telling is a necessary shortcut. To tell is to summarize, to provide exposition, to skim through the action, all of which are appropriate from time to time. We don't need to recount all the moments in a character's life, because only a few of them will be relevant. That means we need to chose which moments to show and which moments to tell.

Say you've got a scene in which a character breaks up with her spouse. After writing the confrontation in great detail, you might tell us, *Marjorie got in her car and drove three hundred miles to the beach, where she spent three days lying in the sun.* We can skim through the drive to the beach and her first three days there because, in this particular story, nothing of consequence happened during that time. But maybe something did happen to Marjorie on her fourth day after the breakup—that's when the showing needs to pick back up again.

Telling tends to become a problem only when you rely on it too much, which typically happens in stories that try to cover a long period of time. The short story form is seldom suitable for epic tales that span generations; it works best in small spaces, spiraling out from a single significant moment in a character's life. The longer the time frame, the greater the pressure to reduce action to summary. The resulting story can end up sounding like the outline for a novel. And though a ten-page version of *War and Peace* might have a certain appeal for the science major wading through a World Literature class, that's not the kind of fiction anyone needs to write.

9
Fact Strangles Fiction

We all write from our own lives—our own views of the world—and the lives we lead provide the raw material we work with. But that's not the same thing as writing autobiographically. If you want to write your own personal story, by all means, do so; creative nonfiction is an important avenue of writing. But if you want to write fiction, you mustn't let "what really happened" interfere with the fiction you're trying to create. Literal truth can become a straight-jacket that keeps you from breaking through into a larger metaphorical truth. The fact that something really happened is never a legitimate excuse to put it in a story. Maybe the act or event you're describing did indeed come to pass in our world, but our world may not be the same one you've communicated on the page. In fact, it can't be. The real world results from the convergence of an infinite number of interconnecting threads that give each moment a context more complex than we can ever imagine. Fiction is only the barest shadow-play of that reality, something cobbled together from a handful of carefully chosen fragments. The context within which our story's action unfolds is necessarily finite. But that's fine—finite fragments are all we need. Fiction isn't about telling the historical truth, it's about fabricating something greater.

10
Theme Provides Focus

First of all, what do we mean by theme? Well, pretty much the same thing you learned in high school. But just because writing theme papers for English class was a chore, don't let that turn you against the value of letting theme shape your creative work now. Theme is the idea the story sets out to explore. It's often the impetus for writing the story. Theme becomes the unifying principle that gives your story intellectual coherence. It functions like the lines of a coloring book that show you where to color; the lines are necessary to remind you that what you're coloring is a clown and not a dinosaur, a farmhouse and not a sailboat.

Awareness of theme is what keeps us from wandering aimlessly in one wrong direction after another. It's the *aboutness* of a story, and without that, there's no dramatic unity, no way to determine what belongs in the story and what doesn't. Aristotle was a big believer in dramatic unity, and so am I. Without dramatic unity, there's no focus, no clear story. We can end up pointlessly passing time with characters instead of accompanying them through a rising action line toward a culminating point of resolution. If you don't know what you're writing about—what general notions you have set out to explore—then your story will probably be intellectually empty.

11
Genre Isn't Inferior

At least not by nature. A lot of genre writers are battle-ready over this point. It's true that sci-fi, romance, westerns, mystery novels and the like have received a lot of bad press in high school and university classrooms for decades. That's because many of those genres grew out of the "dime novel" tradition of early pulp fiction. As a consequence, the Academy has been slow to allow genre-based material into the accepted canon of great literature. But over the last generation the canon has exploded, and it's time for even the most conservative of scholastic institutions to take a closer look at what's out there.

Much of the so-called disreputable nature of genre writing stems from one basic confusion: for decades the terms *genre* and *formula* were interchangeable. Those who would trash genre writing are really trashing formula writing. The fault lies not within any genre, but within the writers who are churning out crappy formula-based examples of a genre.

In a very real sense, genre fiction is a victim of its own success. When there's a huge market for a genre, a lot of superficial versions of it will be pumped into the marketplace. That's the problematic side-effect of popularity—high demand opens the door for inferior works.

Let's not forget that literary fiction is itself a genre;

and as every literary editor knows, only about one submission in a hundred is good enough. That one will get published; the rest won't, except through editorial blunder. The same ratio probably holds true for science fiction, detective stories and the rest—only one in a hundred is worthy of publication. But because the readership demand is high for certain genres, a great deal of the weaker work also finds its way into print. When the majority of published work in a genre is inferior, the reputation of the genre suffers.

But every genre has true artists: Ursula Le Guin in science fiction, Dashiell Hammett in mystery writing, Larry McMurtry in westerns, the Brontë sisters or Jane Austen in romance. The problem is that for each great genre writer, there are dozens of hacks cranking out repetitious formula novels.

So how can you know if your genre story is literary or not? Well, if you're discovering your way forward by exploring an interesting premise, and if the inner lives of the characters matter more than the ray guns they use to blow up the evil aliens, you're probably on solid ground. But if you've outlined the thing beforehand and the writing is just an extended game of connect-the-dots, then you probably aren't creating anything remarkable enough to endure as literature.

12
Questions Create Momentum

Any time you give the reader something to wonder about, you're building suspense, and suspense is simply the state of wondering, of looking forward, on the part of the reader. F. Scott Fitzgerald put it this way: *Draw your chair up close to the edge of the precipice and I'll tell you a story.* The reader wants to teeter on that precipice, to be off balance in a state of worry, or at least a state of questioning. The reader keeps reading to find out the answers to whatever questions you've raised.

But note: you shouldn't frustrate the reader by withholding answers too long. Momentum is generated by constantly raising new questions while answering the old ones.

Say your story starts with a broken window. *Who broke the window?* Ah, it was Billy. *But why?* Well, he was reacting to the news. *What news?* The news about his brother. *Which brother?* Tom, the good brother. *What happened to Tom?* He was in an accident. *What kind of accident?* He drove his car into a tree. *How did it happen?* We don't know yet. *Was he killed?* No, but the others were. *Who were the others?* There've been conflicting reports.

And so on. Lay the trail of breadcrumbs and the reader will follow like a hungry bird. The goal is to keep the reader engaged by each fresh discovery, yet also excited about what may be coming next.

13
Failure Is Normal

It doesn't matter whether you've published ten novels or only a single short story in the *Podunk Review*, all serious artists feel that they're constantly falling short of their goals. I'm sure there are Nobel laureates insecure about what they've accomplished. F. Scott Fitzgerald died thinking himself a failure because his books had gone out of print. No matter how far along the path we may have advanced, the next project always starts with a blank page and an unknown destination, with no guarantee that this book or story will be as good as what we wrote yesterday, or last month, or last year.

Ours is an imperfect art. We don't have the luxury of basic mathematics, in which the columns of numbers either add up or they don't. For us, as in all art, improvement is not an unbroken chain of progress. Tomorrow you may write the best thing you've ever written. Then the next thing you write may stink so badly you'll feel like you don't know anything at all. That's why the only real failure is quitting. Perseverance is what separates the real writers from the talented dilettantes.

14
Head Plus Heart

We're all gifted in different ways. Some people write from the head, others write from the heart. It isn't so much a matter of choice; we simply all have our own natural inclination toward one end of the writing spectrum or the other. There's no value judgment attached—head and heart are equally valid approaches—though as readers or writers we may find our tastes do dictate a preference.

Those who write from the heart might generate a good gush of emotion on the page, getting the reader caught up in—and experiencing—those feelings. Content for such writers matters more than form. Move a reader to tears and you've done your job well.

At the other end of the spectrum, those who write from the head aim to give readers something to think about or to react to intellectually. They may be more concerned with form and structure, especially on the sentence level—as in comedic writing, which depends on timing and word choice. There might be a hundred ways to write a sentence, but only one of them will be funny, and identifying the right combination of words to unlock laughter is more an intellectual exercise than an emotional one.

On the other hand, those who write romance or tragedy usually work from the heart. Of the hundred different ways to write a sentence telling us the puppy is dead, almost all of them will still be sad. Strong emotion arising from a tragic turn of events is less reliant on precision of word choice than it is on honesty of expression.

On an elementary level, the distinction between head

and heart is the distinction between Classicism and Romanticism. The difference is perhaps easier to recognize in poetry: the writer of free verse is by definition less constricted by the specifics of form than the writer of formal verse. William Wordsworth, first of the Romantic poets and the first to experiment with blank verse, proclaimed that the best poetry came as the "spontaneous overflow of powerful feelings." Blank verse more readily accommodates that spontaneous gush of emotion, while a formally constructed sonnet demands the intellectual game of crafting language that conforms to a predetermined architecture—fourteen lines of iambic pentameter with a strictly regulated rhyme scheme.

As I said, we're all somewhere along the spectrum between the two extremes. But it needn't be an either/or proposition. We're all a slightly different mix of head and heart. Here's my advice to make yourself a better writer: first, figure out at which end of the spectrum your natural talent lies; second, try to move your work in the other direction. If you naturally lead with emotion, try to bring in more intellect, more precision of craft. If you naturally write from a place of intellect, try to bring in more spontaneous emotion and lyricism. The best writing is a balance of head and heart, of intellect and emotion. If your stories can make a reader both think and feel, then your work will stand a far better chance of being remembered.

15
Keep Fragments Brief

Many of us are drawn to the sentence fragment. It's a relief to break free from time to time of the bonds of grammar and syntax. Fragments can be an effective—and natural—form of character expression, and they can introduce variety into the rhythms of your prose. But keep fragments brief. Five or six clear, pithy words. Or fewer. The fragment should be something the reader can grasp at a glance.

Each semester I encounter students who use fragments that stretch on for thirty, forty, or fifty words. Why is that a problem? When a fragment is long, the reader doesn't immediately recognize it as a fragment, and that means reading it with the expectation that it'll conform to the rules of grammar and syntax. Thus, when the reader reaches the end and the string of phrases doesn't coalesce into an actual sentence, the immediate impulse is to think the sentence has been misread. So the reader stops and rereads it, looking for his or her mistake. That destroys the flow of the story. You've just forced your reader to interrupt the reading, to step outside the story to look for errors, and that breaks the spell. Never make your reader go back to decipher your sentences.

16
Lift Imaginary Weights

Well, that sounds like a waste of time. But here's what I mean. The imagination acts like a muscle, and if you don't use it, it atrophies. And whether you realize it or not, using your imagination is hard work. Maintaining focus and sustaining what amounts to an artificial dream state while you're writing is physically taxing. It burns energy.

If you sit down to start a writing project after a long dry period, you might easily feel exhausted after writing for an hour. But the next day, you might find you can go a little longer before collapsing, and even longer the day after that. Pretty soon you're writing for three hours without feeling the burn, then four hours, then six, then eight or ten. Within a couple of weeks, you might find yourself able to write twelve hours a day without breaking a sweat. That's because you've *imagined* your way back into writing shape.

There are a couple of lessons in this. First, if you sit down to write and feel exhausted after only a little while, don't despair. Just keep at it, and soon enough your imagination will shake off the rust and you'll be disappearing into full days of writing (if your life allows it). The other lesson, for those capable of sustaining the discipline, is to train yourself never to tune out the imagination in the first place. Carry a notebook, and write down whatever occurs to you that's worth writing down.

I'd bet fifty cents that you've had the following experience: you're going through your day, doing something mundane or interesting or dull or exciting, it doesn't matter what, and suddenly, for no identifiable reason, you have a special thought. Maybe it's an insight. Maybe it's a clever phrase or a lovely sentence. Maybe it's a concept that seems to burn with possibility. It's like the proverbial lightbulb has begun to glow brightly over your head. And what do you do? You tell yourself that you'll certainly write that down later. And what happens later? You can't quite recall the exact language of your glittering phrase. That concept doesn't seem as clear or as fresh, and you don't know why you wanted to write it down in the first place. The whole thing—whatever it was—has dissipated like a dream.

Creativity delayed is creativity denied. That's more than three words, but it's still worthy of a tee-shirt. Seize creativity when it first bubbles up in your mind, because if you don't, it'll vanish, evaporate like morning mist. If you don't respond to it immediately, if you continue to ignore your creative impulse, pretty soon your brain, or your spirit, or whatever it is that's your conduit to the creative realm will learn what you're teaching it: namely, that those insights, special phrases, and bright concepts don't really matter. Then you won't have to bother with them anymore, because they'll stop coming around. Your brain will regard them as spam and send them straight to your mind's recycling bin.

17
People, Not Puppets

Or another three-word way to put it is this: *action requires motive.* Sure, you can make your characters do anything you want them to. Jimmy can celebrate his eighth birthday by hugging Grandma, then sharing his birthday cake with a neighbor kid, then pulling the legs off his pet turtle, then growing a second head. Then he can build a rocket ship in the basement and fly to Mars. How are such things possible? Because whatever you say goes. You're the magical wizard of the story, after all, and nothing falls outside the realm of what you can make happen.

Well, no. You're no more a wizard than the man behind the curtain in Oz. If you're trying to write realistic fiction, you can't violate behavioral reality without destroying the realism you're trying to create. Characters have to act within the context you've given them. Jimmy can't throw a rock at a dog or give his allowance to a homeless man unless you give him a reason to do it. Even if he has a reason, the action has to be consistent with the kind of person you've created him to be. Every action has to come not from the author's need to advance the plot, but from the character's own inner life or backstory. Otherwise the character won't be flesh and blood, it'll just be a wooden marionette manipulated by strings, a ventriloquist's dummy, a puppet. Remember that Pinocchio was of no interest to anyone until he became a living thing, driven by his own passions and desires.

18
Titles Tell Stories

A title is like the handle on a suitcase. It gives the reader something to hold on to, something to make the story transportable. But it also helps the writer. A title—even if it's just a working title—can give you a practical guide, a touchstone, a reference point to refer back to as you blindly grope your way forward through the process of discovering the tale.

Perhaps most important of all is the title's ability to add layers of meaning to a story. Imagine a story of a happy young couple completely in love. Everything they do is sappy and romantic, lots of kissing, lots of cooing and wooing and kind words all around. Title that story "True Love" and you've got a dull cliché on your hands. But title it "The Seeds of Divorce" and suddenly the reader will begin to look more closely at every detail. What seemed initially to be a chirpy romance suddenly takes on darker overtones, and the simple gesture of giving a box of chocolates on Valentine's Day carries the potential for heartache somewhere down the road. With the right title, the most mundane characters and situations can take on unexpected depth and significance.

19
Raise the Stakes

What happens in a story has to matter. The character or characters you've chosen to write about should be at some crossroads in their lives—either physically, emotionally, or psychologically. Otherwise, there's no real reason to focus on the time frame you've chosen. Readers don't want to read about Eddie's normal life, they want to read about the day his life became extraordinary—when he won the lottery, or was attacked on the street by a monkey, or invented a better widget, or caught his wife in the tool shed with the mailman. As the writer, you're free to choose any episode in Eddie's life to present to us, so there needs to be a compelling reason for selecting the one that houses the story. Ideally, it should be an episode that changed Eddie forever, that gave him an entirely new perspective.

To that end, you need to make Eddie's world a complicated one, with problems or pressures crowding in from all sides. In other words, make Eddie's experience true to life. If someone is having trouble paying his mortgage, for example, the bank is probably not his only source of concern. He's probably feeling pressure from his wife and kids to keep the family safe, and he may have employment worries that caused the mortgage crisis in the first place. Maybe he has a gambling problem. Maybe his health is failing. Maybe he needs to have his son's aged dog put to sleep. Maybe there's a crack in the foundation of the house and water is leaking into the basement. Maybe there's a nest of hornets outside the back door. Maybe he's coping with feelings of failure, believing his parents will be ashamed of him. Maybe he's an alcoholic on the wagon. The possibilities are endless.

Don't pile on so many problems that the effect becomes comic, however. Too much tragedy can start to seem ridiculous. But don't give your people smooth sailing. The well-being of any main character needs to be at risk, or else we'll never take a rooting interest in his or her predicament.

20
Chisel or Gush

Well, that's not really an aphorism, so this one might not belong on a tee-shirt, but it's still something I want to bring up. It's about *how* we write.

When I was in graduate school, back in the horse-and-buggy days, I could generate upwards of thirty pages in a late-night session on my cutting-edge Smith-Corona portable electric typewriter. In those days I was what you might call a gusher, spewing out an unbroken stream of language in pursuit of whatever story I was trying to capture. Ever forward, no looking back, no speed bumps, that was my approach. A "story" was whatever I could manage to crank out in a single sitting.

Most writers tend to start out that way, I think. Maybe it's the template we align ourselves to in high school and college, when we have to churn out that English lit paper the night before it's due. I've seen countless stories in my writing classes that were obviously the result of a last-minute all-nighter.

Some writers continue to write that way because for them it works. We're all different critters, and we each have to find the style that suits us best. But for me, gushing was the wrong approach. All my "stories" turned out to be meandering forays into empty territory. I was just spinning my wheels.

The thing is, I knew I was generating crap even as I was writing it. Sometimes I knew it as early as the second sentence, but I'd always tell myself, *I'll go back and fix it later.* But later, when I returned to the scene of the crime to repair whatever misstep I'd made in that second sentence, I'd find that by fixing that second sentence, the story took on a new direction, and everything I'd written in the remaining thirty pages was rendered irrelevant.

My turning point came when a car in which I was a passenger broke down on a country road in Indiana. The other passenger was the great Southern writer Reynolds Price, and while the owner of the car, who was the director of the graduate program in which I was enrolled, hiked back into town for gas, I was charged with keeping Mr. Price company. I got to talk craft with the man for a couple of hours, which probably bored the hell out of him but did me a lot of good. At one point I asked him how many pages he could generate in a day. This guy was a pro, so I figured he could give me a good idea of how much I needed to elevate my page count to enter the big leagues. He thought about the question for a while and told me that on a really productive twelve-hour day of writing, sometimes he could generate upwards of three pages.

What? Three pages? That was less than one word per

minute. What was wrong with him? Did he type with his elbows? How could a famous writer be so slow?

Slow, of course, wasn't the right word for it, as I eventually realized. Meticulous, that was closer to it. Precise. Discerning. Artistically rigorous on the microscopic level.

That approach might not be for everybody, but I discovered it was the right approach for me. Now I can be thrilled if, in a twelve-hour day of writing, I can chisel out two pages worth keeping. But even a single salvageable paragraph can make me happy. I've discovered once and for all that, given the two options, I'm a chiseler, not a gusher.

It's up to you to find your own most efficient way to work—whether it suits you better to move slowly, revising every sentence as you go, or to go back later and revise, after you've already crossed that temporary finish line of a draft.

At heart, the gusher is driven by the need to see, as soon as possible, the rough shape of the story. The chiseler, on the other hand, initially places more focus on the smaller building blocks—the sentences. While the gusher begins with the macroscopic, postponing the microscopic concerns until later, the chiseler starts with the microscopic and inches a way forward, word by word, toward the larger, more macroscopic concerns. Either way can work, depending on the predilections of the writer.

I bring up this duality of styles because often, when we're starting out, it never occurs to us that there might be an entirely different way to approach the craft. If you're working in one of these modes and you feel you're not getting the results you want, try the other. Maybe, like me, you'll have a breakthrough.

So: that's twenty three-word phrases relevant to your development as a writer. Of course there are many others. *Don't waste words* might be one. *Maintain your POV* another. *Avoid adjectival overload* is one I wrestled with early on.

But the best three words of all might simply be *Revise, revise, revise.* Revision is both our weapon and our shield, and the more we use it, the more powerful it becomes. Revision is what saves the work from calamity and us from humiliation. With enough revision, you actually *can* make a silk purse out of a sow's ear.

Luckily, I'm at least savvy enough to know I don't have all the answers, so the last three-word dictum I'll leave you with is the one that carries the greatest potential: *This space available.* Fill in the space with some guiding principle of your own, something that speaks to a weakness you've identified in your own writing. We all have shortcomings in our craft, and I've just given you a lengthy list of ones I've discovered in my own work over the decades. Your list will no doubt be different from mine, but there's bound to be a lot of overlap. And one thing I've learned from committing so many missteps in my day is that I can't fix a problem until I've identified it.

Of course, *This space available* has another application, too. That's the message the blank page is giving us every time we sit down to write. It's an invitation. Don't be shy about accepting.

10

INSPIRATION/WRITER'S BLOCK

Story, Image, and Idea

Writer's block descends upon us all at one time or another. Nobody knows why. Ability seems to have nothing to do with it. Maybe our imaginations operate like a hot water tank: we turn on the faucet and the creativity flows—until the tank runs cold. Then we have to wait for the next tankful to heat up.

But what if we keep waiting and nothing happens? What if there's a massive power outage in wintertime, and the water in the tank freezes over? What if our imaginations stay stuck?

I've known great writers who, inexplicably, suffered through years of writer's block. I've known others who spiraled into panic if a single unimaginative week passed by. The response will vary from writer to writer. Some sink into passive acceptance, some get angry, some get depressed. Some try craft exercises. Some meditate. Some, sadly, try to kickstart the creative juices through drugs or alcohol. Some seek out adventure, á la Hemingway, pushing themselves toward danger as if adrenaline were somehow connected to the act of writing.

First of all, I do believe it's natural to go through periods of incubation. But natural or not, the experience can make us antsy. At some point, if the incubation drags on too long, we may even think we're washed up as writers.

But there are ways to overcome times of stagnation that don't involve back-alley drug deals or the juggling of chainsaws. The late poet William Stafford once told me that he'd discovered the definitive cure. "I just lower my standards," he said. That may do it for many people. Bad writing is far easier to revise than a blank page—and even the most talented and experienced among us are capable of bad writing.

My own solution takes a different route. I read other writers. Some people balk at that idea, I know. They get caught up in the anxiety of influence, fearing that if they read other writers, they'll start sounding like those other writers rather than themselves.

But influence is nothing to be afraid of. In fact, it's a necessary stage of learning the craft. It's true that we can't help being influenced by those writers we admire, but we're also influenced by writers we don't like, because they teach us what not to do. Without knowledge of other writers, without the balancing influence of their work to guide us, we would be writing in ignorance and darkness.

My own path out of that darkness is built upon three mainstays of the craft: story, image, and idea. Long before I learned to read, I was fascinated by story, captivated by image, and enthralled with idea. In those early, formative days, when I was being read to by adults, story gave me scenarios, often magical, that opened up infinite possibilities about the world.

Image gave me pictures, also magical, which I could conjure in my own imagination long after the story had ended. Idea gave me other ideas—because that's what thinking does, it gives rise to more thinking, creating a chain of interlocking ideas that form one's vision of the world. Give a child an idea, and you will set his or her mind in motion.

In my case, the earliest examples of story, image, and idea came from a bare handful of sources, all of them in poetry. First, there was mysterious Mother Goose, with her cast of fanciful characters—Humpty Dumpty, Wee Willie Winkie, Jack and Jill, Three Blind Mice, and the rest—all of them spurs to the imagination.

From Mother Goose I moved on to the poems of Robert Louis Stevenson, a master of story, image, and idea. His collection, *A Child's Garden of Verses,* introduced me to metaphor and made the daily details of my preschool existence seem to matter. And in writing about a child's dreams, he summed up the fleeting nature of creativity itself:

> Try as I might to find the way,
> I never can get back by day,
> Nor can remember plain and clear
> The curious music that I hear.

Next in my education—and for many of my generation—came Rudyard Kipling. His poem "Gunga Din" was the first piece of literature I ever encountered that created a lower-class character voice—that of a Cockney British soldier. As a child in the pre-enlightened Deep South, I was affected by the content of the poem. The story, you'll remember, takes place during the time of British Imperial expansion; specifically, the occupation of India. Gunga Din was the much abused water carrier who brought nourishment to the British troops on the front line. The soldiers treated him as something less than human because of his perceived racial inferiority—until he sacrificed his life in their service. Most will recall the ending of that poem:

> Though I've belted you and flayed you,
> By the livin' Gawd that made you,
> You're a better man than I am, Gunga Din.

From the first time I read that Kipling poem, I never forgot the powerful story, the gruesome imagery, or the idea of human equality underlying the tale. This particular piece of art, this single poem, raised my awareness about the injustice of judging people by their race. To whatever degree I was able to escape the rampant bigotry of the culture I grew up in, that poem may account for a good portion of it. It gave me a better ideal to live up to than some of the examples I saw in the Alabama classrooms and neighborhoods of the 1950s and early 1960s. Without poetry I might have wound up just one more benighted redneck with a gun rack in my truck.

I'm telling you about the poems I read as a child because I suspect that you may have had a similar experience. Much of the literature of childhood is poetry—from Mother Goose to Dr. Seuss. Poetry is quite possibly at the heart of what first inspired you to write. I would also guess that the first pieces of writing you ever memorized were passages of poetry. We *read* stories. We *learn* poems. They are, and will always be, sources of inspiration and delight.

For good reason. Narrative poetry often contains what a good piece of fiction has, and more. *The Iliad* and *The Odyssey* would have been great novels but for the fact that they're poems. Lyric poetry is a little more fleeting, giving us a portrait, a sketch, a circumstance, a feeling—reducing story to a snapshot, like a piece of flash fiction. If the snapshot is well-executed, we'll get a full experience, and short poems can convey large stories.

Poetry was a common training ground where we learned—consciously or not—the importance of story, image, and idea. In my case, I can say that poetry taught me how to write fiction. And even today, poetry remains my best avenue into prose. If I'm stuck in a section of a fiction manuscript, I'll turn away from what I'm working on and pick up a volume of poetry. Pretty soon, worlds begin to open up, just as they did when I was five. Story notions occur to me. Images rise up in my imagination. I discover a line of thinking that I want to investigate, some unanswerable question that's worth pondering. I go through *What if?* after *What if?* until I hit upon something fresh enough to arrest my ongoing attention. Poetry rekindles the fire, and all I have to do is go back to my piece of prose, filled with new energy. Poetry inspires.

So if you should find yourself languishing in a bad case of writer's block, I'd encourage you to return to those roots and let poetry be your avenue back to writing fiction. After all, it's worked for some of the great heavyweights. We all know that Shakespeare wrote poetry. Sir Walter Scott, inventor of the historical novel, owed his first allegiance to poetry. Thomas Hardy, while more famous for his hefty novels, was one of the leading poets of his age. In 1947 Robert Penn Warren won the Pulitzer Prize for his novel *All the King's Men,* but poetry was his greater love; in 1958 he won the Pulitzer Prize in poetry, becoming the only writer to win that award in both categories. Margaret Atwood is both a poet and a fiction writer. John Updike, two-time winner of the Pulitzer Prize in fiction, was also a dedicated poet; his first published book was a collection of poems, as was his last. Raymond Carver, the most prominent short story writer of the last fifty years, started out as a poet, and his final book, like Updike's, was a collection of poems. All of these fiction writers nurtured their creativity through poetry, whether writing it, reading it, or both.

In short, poetry can inspire you, and inspiration is the best antidote I know to writer's block.

But what, specifically, does poetry have to teach us about fiction? Well, to begin with, in narrative poems the story is distilled down to its purest essence. There's dramatic unity, meaning that everything in the poem is relevant—as it should be in a piece of fiction. If a scene or action doesn't relate in some way to the story at hand, it's a digression that belongs elsewhere, in some story other than the one you're writing. This is a mistake I see in many beginning novelists. They seem to think they have to put their entire world experience into the novel, as if it's the only book they're ever going to write. It's okay, and even advisable, to save something for the second novel, and the third.

Poetry also shows us the virtue of Aristotle's observation that the story should be told from as far along the action line as possible. In Melville's *Moby Dick,* for example, the author knows there's no reason to develop lengthy scenes about Ishmael's grammar school sweetheart or his trouble with arithmetic, or the morning he lost his hat in the outhouse, or whatever else he might have experienced before he set foot on the *Pequod.* What happened on the ill-fated voyage with Ahab is what matters, so that's where the story unfolds.

The story of your short fiction or novel should be specifically focused on the time frame of greatest action and significance. Cut that useless runway of material you've probably tacked onto the front of your narrative. Find the *poem* in your character's story—which is to say, find the heart of it, and begin right there.

Now, as to image, that's at the core of your selection of scenes. Every scene should serve a specific purpose in the narrative, and every scene needs to be made memorable with concrete details and action. Images.

When we recall the famous scenes from literature, they're virtually all rooted in an image. Scrooge time-traveling with his ghosts. Ahab plunging his harpoon into Moby Dick. Anna Karinina throwing herself under the train. The image doesn't have to be that active, though. In Dickens' *A Tale of Two Cities* the enduring image, besides the guillotine, is that of Madame Defarge sitting ominously in a chair, knitting.

Every great work of literature will have enduring images. A man in a white suit staring across a body of water toward a green light on a dock—that has to be from the world of *The Great Gatsby.* Prisoners of war picking through the rubble of a devastated city for salvage while their German guards hover over them—that has to be Vonnegut's *Slaughterhouse Five*. An old bloody-handed fisherman in a small boat on the open sea—obviously that's Hemingway's *The Old Man and the Sea*. A man in torment on his knees, covering his ears, with a dead body under the floorboards beneath him—that's Poe's "The Telltale Heart." An old woman sitting in a ditch at edge of the woods beside a younger man with a pistol pointed at her chest—that's Flannery O'Connor's "A Good Man Is Hard to Find."

Every one of these scenes is memorable—first, because the writer has taken the time to give us enough details to make the scene come alive in our imaginations; and second, because of the action surrounding the image. Each image is a marker for something important that has just happened or is about to happen. All your scenes should have that kind of specific poetic magnitude. Otherwise, we won't remember them. And if we won't remember a scene, why have you bothered to write it?

That's an easy test to apply to any scene you write: *Does it have poetic magnitude?*

One of the most common errors I see in stories and novels is the clichéd opening of the character waking up in the morning. Perhaps the writer has chosen the right day in the character's life upon which to hang the tale, but that doesn't mean we need the entire day from beginning to end. Skip the morning rituals, the showering and brushing of teeth, the drinking of the morning coffee and the eating of corn flakes or a muffin. Jump to the moment when the long-lost brother enters the store where the character works. Or the moment when the character walks through the hospital room door and sees her father for the first time since the stroke. Or the moment when the mother finds the drug paraphernalia in her son's dresser drawer. What the hell does breakfast have to do with any of that? We won't care about breakfast. We won't remember it. So don't write it.

Or if you insist on taking us through the breakfast experience, make it unlike any breakfast we've ever witnessed. Give us images that will stick in our minds. Put an armadillo under the kitchen table. Have the toaster set fire to the curtains above the sink. Have a stranger walk in and pour himself a bowl of those corn flakes and sit down across from your baffled main character.

Every scene needs tension, uncertainty, the possibility for disaster. Otherwise, the scene will become a stopping point where the reader will be free to put down the book and go find something more interesting to do. It's your job to reward the reader with something interesting every step of the way. Fail to do that, and you will have wasted everyone's time, including your own.

And finally: idea. This is a tricky area to talk about. Idea can often be confused with message, and good art will rarely carry an overt message, because messages are propaganda, even if we agree with them. Art should encourage thought, rather than tell us what to think.

Sometimes, of course, a work can rise above the limits of its propaganda. The great religious paintings of the Renaissance, for example, often hammered home a specific Christian message. The film script for *Casablanca* was one of the greatest ever written, but it contained a heavy-handed strand of propaganda, denouncing American isolationism and promoting the French-American partnership in World War II. Luckily, it also had other story lines going for it that were separate from the political theme it was pushing, most notably the love story between Rick and Ilsa—though Ilsa doesn't appear until more than a half hour into the film. As a general rule, though, people don't like being preached to, so if you want to write just to promote a message, better stick to email, blogging, or your Facebook page. Poetry and fiction thrive as explorations, rather than as soapbox lectures or stump speeches. Didactic art—art that tells us what to think—is far less enduring than art which raises questions and invites us to think for ourselves.

To that end, I'd suggest that your stories should be an investigation of some idea, some notion that baffles or intrigues you. Write to explore or discover, not to tell us what you think you already know.

Idea, sometimes called theme in a story or novel, is also a means of keeping your focus, as I've noted earlier. Ask yourself how each scene you write reveals some aspect of your theme that you haven't explored before. If you can't answer that question, then the scene has no justification for its existence. If the scene merely rehashes some avenue of thought you've already covered, then the scene is redundant and should be cut. If your only defense is that the scene is interesting, that may not be reason enough to include it. Save such interesting digressions for a story in which that scene can be the star, rather than a mere bit player filling in the background.

As I've said before, I believe that every good work of literary art needs an "aboutness." If the work isn't about anything, it's empty, and empty art is no art at all. The aboutness of fiction is where the idea dwells.

Think of the idea as the life-enriching gift you're trying to deliver to your reader. The images you use are the packaging that protects it while it's in transport. The story is the delivery system that conveys your idea to households all across the country and the world—or at least to those few folks who still appreciate literature.

More often than not, a poem is something that's well-crafted, as opposed to something that's just dashed off in a gush of enthusiasm. So too should a piece of fiction be something that's labored over, with attention paid to every word on the page. It should be built from language that flows seamlessly from one sentence to the next. It should have rhythm and a sense of pace. It should reveal information in the most productive ways. It should reach out both to the mind and the heart. Above all, it should have musicality to it—the same music we once tried to recall from our young, enchanted dreams.

Acknowledgments

"Story, Image, and Idea" first appeared in *Hunger Mountain*

"Mr. Potato Head vs. Freud" first appeared in *The Writer's Chronicle*

My thanks to the Vermont College of Fine Arts for providing a venue for the lectures which provided the foundation for these essays; and to Virginia Commonwealth University, for assembling a great MFA program in which I am fortunate enough to work; and to the many students who encouraged me to write this book, Amber Timmerman chief among them.

My thanks as well to Keith Ratzlaff, Jeff Gundy, David Wojahn, David Jauss, Bret Lott, Kevin Morgan Watson, Jim Peterson, and Curt Musselman & Cecelia Brown, who together have given me over two hundred years of solid friendship and support.

And to Dawn Cooper, for just about everything.

Note on the Author

Clint McCown has taught for over forty-five years at some of the country's top schools and writing programs, including Virginia Commonwealth University, the Vermont College of Fine Arts, Wake Forest University, the University of Alabama, Beloit College, the Stonecoast MFA Program, and Indiana University. His works of fiction include the novels *Haints* (winner of the Midwest Book Award), *The Member-Guest* (winner of the Society of Midland Authors Award), *The Weatherman* (winner of the S. Mariella Gable Prize), and *War Memorials,* as well as the short story collection, *Music for Hard Times: New & Selected Stories.* The only two-time winner of the American Fiction Prize, he has also received an NEA grant, a Distinction in Literature citation from the Wisconsin Library Association, a Barnes & Noble *Great New Writer* designation, the Germaine Breé Book Award, an Academy of American Poets Prize, and an Associated Press Award for Documentary Excellence for his investigations of political corruption and organized crime. His work has appeared in such places as *Sewanee Review, North American Review, Gettysburg Review, The Southern Review, Northwest Review, Mississippi Review, Colorado Review, Kansas Quarterly, Alaska Quarterly, America, Golf Digest, Hotel Amerika, Richmond Noir, Hunger Mountain,* and scores of other journals. He is a former editor of *Indiana Review* and was the founder of the *Beloit Fiction Journal,* which he edited for twenty years. Additionally, he has published five collections of poems, and he has received three Notable Essay citations in the *Best American Essays* series. For four years he served as General Editor for the AWP Intro Journals Awards, and he currently serves as a contributing editor for *Colorado Review.* He has also worked as a screenwriter for Warner Bros., as a Creative Consultant for HBO television, and as a principal actor with the National Shakespeare Company. In 2021 he was inducted into the Writers Hall of Fame at Wake Forest University.

www.ingramcontent.com/pod-product-compliance
Lightning Source LLC
LaVergne TN
LVHW051001080826
845145LV00009B/2399

* 9 7 8 1 9 5 0 4 1 3 3 9 3 *